PRAISE FOR ESTRANGED

"Susan's book confirms that our friendships should evolve as we do and reminds us not to get stuck in patterns of obligation or expectation. The questions she asks readers to consider will help those struggling with a relationship while also strengthening their own self-worth."
—Janet Sherlund, author, *Abandoned at Birth*

"Any woman who's experienced the disappointment of a broken friendship will find empathy, solace, and encouragement in this book. Through many interviews, with a professional's perspective on the complexities of female relationships, Susan Shapiro Barash brings new understanding to the myriad consequences of failed friendships."
—Diane Parrish, author of *Something Better*

PRAISE FOR SUSAN SHAPIRO BARASH'S OTHER WORK

[Tripping the Prom Queen]
  "Gracefully interweaves incisive analysis and everyday lessons we could all stand to learn, deepening the conversation about female aggression with an honest voice women will recognize."
  —Rachel Simmons, author of *Odd Girl Out*

[Toxic Friends]
  "Barash skillfully channels her interviewees' experiences and convinces us that these real and raw friendships are the norm."
  —*Publishers Weekly*

[*Little White Lies, Deep Dark Secrets*]
"A fascinating, nonjudgmental look at the unique cultural pressures that reward women for keeping secrets and lying."
—Leslie Morgan Steiner, editor, *Mommy Wars*

[*The Nine Phases of Marriage*]
"A must-read for anyone who wants to understand how we change in marriage and how marriage changes us."
—Meera Lester, author of *The Marriage Devotional*

[*You're Grounded Forever . . . But First Let's Go Shopping*]
"Dives into the true complexity of the mother-daughter relationship . . . Embrace, read, and absorb solutions!"
—Karyl McBride, Ph.D., author of *Will I Ever Be Good Enough?*

[*The New Wife: The Evolving Role of the American Wife*]
"Barash's conclusions are backed by statistics in addition to the interviews and cultural research. The book comes to life with the voices of many candid women and ends all too soon. Recommended for large public and academic libraries."
—*Library Journal*

ESTRANGED

ALSO BY SUSAN SHAPIRO BARASH

A Passion for More: Affairs that Make or Break Us

The Nine Phases of Marriage: How to Make It, Break It, Keep It

You're Grounded Forever, But First Let's Go Shopping

Toxic Friends: The Antidote for Women Stuck in Complicated Friendships

Tripping the Prom Queen: The Truth about Women and Rivalry

Little White Lies, Deep Dark Secrets: The Truth about Why Women Lie

The New Wife: The Evolving Role of the American Wife

Sisters: Devoted or Divided

Second Wives: The Pitfalls and Rewards of Marrying Widowers and Divorced Men

Reclaiming Ourselves: How Women Dispel a Legacy of Bad Choices

Mothers-in-Law and Daughters-in-Law: Love, Hate, Rivalry and Reconciliation

Women of Divorce: Mothers, Daughters, Stepmothers— The New Triangle

FICTION BY SUSANNAH MARREN (PEN NAME)

Between the Tides

A Palm Beach Wife

A Palm Beach Scandal

Maribelle's Shadow

ESTRANGED

How Strained Female Friendships
Are Mended or Ended

SUSAN SHAPIRO BARASH

MERIDIAN EDITIONS

WESTPORT, CONNECTICUT

Copyright © 2025 Susan Shapiro Barash

Published by Meridian Editions
Westport, Connecticut

No part of this book may be reproduced, or stored in a retrieval system, or transmitted in any form or by any means, electronic, mechanical, photocopying, recording, or otherwise, without express written permission of the publisher.

www.susanshapirobarash.com

ISBN (paperback): 978-1-959170-20-4
ISBN (hardcover): 978-1-959170-21-1
ISBN (ebook): 978-1-959170-22-8

Cover and book designed by John Lotte

Manufactured in the U.S.A.

For Women Everywhere

Even loss and betrayal can bring us awakening.

—BUDDHA

CONTENTS

Preface: Has She Changed or Have I?   xv

PART ONE: The Give and Take

Chapter One: **A Faithless Friend**   3
Exhibit A: The Sacrifice   22

Chapter Two: **A Wayward Friend**   32
Exhibit B: Thin Ice: Instability   47

Chapter Three: **A Diametrically Opposed Friend**   57
Exhibit C: Ambitions Collide   76

PART TWO: Toxic Bonds

Chapter Four: **A Flippant Friend**   89
Exhibit D: Untrustworthy   103

Chapter Five: **A Disparaging Friend**   112
Exhibit E: Secrets Spilled   126

Chapter Six: **A Green-eyed Friend**   133
Exhibit F: Double Betrayal   149

Chapter Seven: **A Thieving Friend**   162
Exhibit G: Dicey Triangles   176

PART THREE: **How We Defriend**

    Chapter Eight: **The Breakup/Ghosting**   193
        Exhibit H: Clarity   209

    Chapter Nine: **Successful Estrangements**   216
        Exhibit I: Acceptance   233

    Epilogue: **Owning Our Decisions**   241

Acknowledgments   253

Questionnaire Responses   255

References   261

AUTHOR'S NOTE

This book is based on extensive personal interviews with women and experts in the field of psychology and counseling. Names have been changed and recognizable characteristics disguised of all people in this book except the contributing experts. Some characters are composites.

A NOTE TO THE READER

References in this book to web sites and other resources as potential sources of additional information does not mean that either the author or the publisher endorses anything that might be said in such material. Neither the author nor the publisher has control over, or is responsible for, the content or policies of this material.

PREFACE

Has She Changed or Have I?

Sometimes when I have insomnia, I count the close friends I've made and lost along the way. I see them in a sort of receiving line of missing friends, waiting for me to figure out what went wrong, how our relationships played out, who was at fault and why things soured. At the end of the line is my former best friend, Paulette, who altered the course of my life. The friend who lied about the man I wanted to marry. The friend who stole my chance to be with a person I loved.

Paulette and I had met when we were eleven at a ski resort in Vermont. When we were in graduate school, we lived together. During this time, Jake, my college boyfriend, walked away. No one understood my mourning and sadness as well as Paulette. No one listened to my heartbreak and soothed me more than she. He promised to call only when he was ready to make a commitment. Back then Paulette and I had one black rotary phone in the kitchen. There was no answering machine. We were both on red alert for the Jake call. I still loved him. As far as I knew that call never came.

A year later, I was engaged to someone else. At the rehearsal dinner the night before my wedding, Paulette cornered me. She confessed that Jake *had* called—he had asked her to relay a message and she had decided I didn't need to know. In her opinion, I had moved on. I had begun to date the man I was about to marry. My first reaction was to flee, call the wedding off. Then I thought of my fiancé/soon-to-be-husband, his trust in me. I thought of Paulette, who was my best friend, wasn't she?

The next day she was in my wedding.

The baffling part is that I still wanted Paulette in my life, as close as ever. I somehow excused her, our friendship was that significant. But shouldn't I have left Paulette—weren't her acts flagrant enough? Instead I wasn't able to claim how deeply I was wronged and yearned for her company.

A Road Map for Female Bonds

I'm not the only one who has clung to a close friend, a best friend who has been destructive and unreliable. There are plenty of women who are heavily engaged in their female friendships and have been blindsided. These are serious, significant friendships, not merely 'medium' friendships, as Lisa Miller identifies them in her essay in the *New York Times*, "The Vexing Problem of the 'Medium Friend'." What she writes about are bona fide friends but not inner sanctum friendships. We have fewer rules and expectations for our casual friends and don't hold the bar as high.

For *Estranged,* I am focusing only on women's experiences and only with their most meaningful friends. After all, we view these alliances as a refuge, a 'found family,' a sisterhood built on choice, not assignment. This is where women feel understood, safe and accepted. Each of us knows which friend to seek out for career advice, a medical emergency, for an adventure or a shoulder to cry on. The modeling is everywhere and comes from every direction—our mothers, mentors, celebrity influences, social media, novels, film, and podcasts.

As I began this project, interviewing one hundred and fifty women, diverse in terms of age, race, religion, ethnicity, education, earning power, I realized our deep regrets and how much these friendships matter. And how often women cling to unproductive friendships despite rejection, double-crossing, and misery. Sisters too have their own dramas. Although sisters are from the same family and therefore 'assigned' to each other, while friends choose each other for a variety of reasons, our relationships with our sisters mirror the complexity and depth of our relationships with our friends. The acute sense of loss we experience when a sister bond fractures is the same. Some women report a severed tie to a sister makes their female friendships all the more important with the hope it can fill the emptiness of the estranged sister. Therefore, I have included a sister narrative per chapter of this book.

The strife between female friends starts early. By first grade we know who can be trusted versus who will spill our secrets. As the years go on, who will pilfer your love interest, job or other best friend, who will ditch you to be with the right crowd or for her partner's sake. Over time these disappointments, antagonisms, and hostilities settle in and wind into replay. After a falling out, a betrayal, an aggression, there is still the second-guessing. *That's because the message remains that female friends are worth holding onto.*

There is no official way to end a fruitless friendship. We have been encouraged by our families, mentors and peers to seek out a best friend and close friends to confide in and count on. Famous female feuds have always piqued our interest for that very reason. For example, as reported in the tabloids, Selena Gomez and Demi Lovato, Paris Hilton and Lindsay

Lohan, Paris Hilton and Nicole Richie, Katy Perry and Rihanna, Katy Perry and Taylor Swift, Kylie Jenner and Jordyn Woods. Rivals in their careers, Britney Spears and Christina Aguilera's first falling out as tweens was over Justin Timberlake.

Gossip swirled around the split of Meghan Markle and her best friend Jessica Mulroney. According to *The Daily Mail*, Jessica was Meghan's confidante when she and Harry became engaged and a 'key player' at their 2018 wedding, yet she did not appear in the couple's 2022 docuseries. When news of the *Vanderpump Rules* affair surfaced and Tom Sandoval's and Raquel Leviss's tryst became public, there was great sympathy for Ariana Madix, the injured party. According to *People* magazine, Madix had considered Leviss a friend until the betrayal. In a *Us Weekly* piece, "Taylor Swift's Celebrity BFFs Through the Years" staff editors refer to an 'exclusive squad' that existed in 2010 and how by 2019 she realized some of the friendships were 'situational.'

Decades ago, in a classic public defriending, Elizabeth Taylor and Debbie Reynolds, famed film stars of the 1950s, fell out after Taylor had a fling with Reynolds's husband, Eddie Fisher. Taylor and Fisher married and the two female friends did not reconcile until 1996, according to elizabethtaylor.com.

Sister clashes can mirror best friend clashes. Sam Kashner reports in *Vanity Fair* that Jackie Kennedy and Lee Radziwill were cohesive and competitive. Lee had been in a relationship with Aristotle Onassis for six years only to watch Jackie marry him.

Whatever our reactions for women in the public eye, we can relate to their experiences. How we are drawn to our closest friends echoes a love interest. These bonds offer not only comfort and shared interests, but also a refuge. There is a sense of endless support, a form of unconditional love.

Only these friends will get us through. Until they don't.

She Said/She Said

For the past six years I've been listening to women who dread losing these connections, even if the friend has stolen a friend or work idea or is envious or harshly critical. The friend might have opposing values or be involved in unacceptable behaviors. She may disregard the friendship or allow a stranger to interfere with the bond they share. Some spoke of being in sub-optimal friendships as worse than being defeated in a romance. For others, worse than a divorce. Yet we know the 21st century stats—that our marriages have about a fifty percent chance of survival. We're savvy about the fluidity of relationships—we have finessed changing jobs, lovers, colleagues. We know not to expect things to go on endlessly. Still, we believe it is the female friend who is meant to last. We have been persuaded by societal messaging to be patient and forgiving in these friendships.

Red Flag Friendships

The fact is that friendships shift over time. A treasured friend becomes unavailable, a solid friend seems shaky, differing perspectives become an issue. Still, we are invested in the relationship, we keep at it. As I pulled my notes together, I found seven classic scenarios that lead to disappointment, loss or a breakup:

1. **A Faithless Friend:** This is a friend who was always available but a third party or a circumstance is driving you apart. The friend becomes distant.
2. **A Wayward Friend:** In these distressing situations, women describe the challenges of standing behind a friend who is involved in questionable, possibly dangerous behavior.

3. **A Diametrically Opposed Friend:** Being with a friend and no longer sharing the same values can be slippery. Lately we've seen it in terms of politics, personal beliefs, and worldview.

4. **A Flippant Friend:** If a close friend shows little respect for a particular friend, it's a problem. She could be hierarchal, viewing other friends as more important.

5. **A Disparaging Friend:** Even constructive criticism is hard to handle, but the friend who is deprecating spawns an infective environment.

6. **A Green-eyed Friend:** A friend who is jealous or envious does not wish her friends well. Women say they live in dread, hoping she won't hear their good news, downplaying rather than sharing any successes.

7. **Thieving Friend:** When a friend steals from us, be it a person or a creative idea, it's a multi-level betrayal, one that harms the soul of a friendship.

Awakening

Within this wide sweep of behavior, we come to understand what an ailing, unrewarding friendship can do to our own mental health. There are those of us able to extricate ourselves without remorse or balking. Yet for the most part, women haven't been good at these clean breaks. More likely they become stymied, worrying that a breakup smacks of failure and loss.

We've been encouraged to see what is favorable in these bonds. Shelley E. Taylor, a social neuroscientist and author of

The Tending Instinct, views women's friendship as having a mitigating effect on stress. Women in beneficial friendships have lower blood pressure, their immunity is boosted and they heal better.

The training for females feeds into this—we're expected to be grateful for these ties. We're taught to avoid conflict at any cost, to be demur. It's better to salvage what was once of value. Since there is simply no official way to end a futile friendship, we soldier on, in unfulfilling or even injurious situations. We are without the notion of an 'adult time out' or a recognized form of detachment (as divorce is to a deficient marriage). There is no 'how to' manual that would ease our misgivings and self-blame. The idea of losing a friend creates great anxiety; it's a tough concept to digest. We need these ties and when they go astray, we suffer.

To this point, it's no surprise that traditionally, women have hung in, willing to ignore grievances big and small. Obviously, based on my friendship with Paulette—one that spanned decades before the denouement that I'll share with you in the coming pages—I had contorted myself to keep it going.

The idea of escape, of ditching unsatisfactory female friends, has been in the ether. Today, in a bold step, we are amplifying our desire for rewarding friends. This shift has occurred in several phases. Partly it accelerated as a Covid 'wakeup' and a mode of self-care. Yet it had been in the works before that. As women have flourished in their careers and have grown more confident in their romantic lives, they have become less vulnerable. As they have celebrated their achievements and earning power, they have become less needy with more clarity.

Although few of us want to be without our closest friends, there can be simmering injustices and recurring dramas in the mix. Women report imagining life without the friend who churns up trouble and causes psychic pain. Our efforts to escape an outright end might include avoidance, making excuses, ghosting and a slow fade. And friends who instigate the breakup report being as anguished as the friends they leave behind. What is in play is the risk of leaving versus the risk of staying.

The Best Path Forward

Most recently I have been hearing from women who let go of suboptimal friends and did this with confidence, protecting themselves and overcoming the misery as they moved on. Instead of the usual rationalizing—a fear of cancel culture and separating—they thoughtfully distance from the friendship without severing themselves from it. They remain in contact but not close. This step taken is a survival mechanism, a form of resilience that sets them free to develop rewarding future connections. For others estrangement becomes the answer. In this study we will consider how each action affects us. The outcomes are that women leave with a sense of purpose. My research reveals:

> 88% of women have had a problem with a close friend.
>
> 75% feel more obligated to stay with a female friend than a partner or husband.
>
> 61% have had a friend who has done something terrible to them.
>
> 63% have had a friend break up with them.
>
> 67% have wanted to leave a friend behind.

75% have left a friend and felt relieved.

72% have had the courage to break up with a female friend.

79% found that becoming estranged is positive.

Estranged offers steps toward a future with sturdy bonds and self-respect. I have detailed the repercussions and advantages of estrangement, after women emerged more in touch with their own needs and expectations.

By looking beyond the conventional view, where women feel wounded and defeated, there is a sense of victory and agency. In this paradigm, women carefully instigate and finesse the procedure and result. They make the decision to renegotiate, regroup or move on. Bypassing the consequences of a rift with a female friend, they have the guts to exit, if they so choose. They've navigated this difficult task and have kindly shared the details.

No wonder I was compelled to write this book.

PART ONE

The Give and Take

CHAPTER ONE

A Faithless Friend

> Are you on edge at times because the friendship doesn't feel secure?
>
> Is this friend someone who is there for you unless something more important comes along?
>
> Do you second-guess yourself when you are with her?
>
> Can she be icy out of nowhere?
>
> Have you noticed how you rationalize both her behavior and yours?

If this is the case, then you are in a friendship where you have considered leaving but have resisted:

> You should have seen it coming, you've suspected your best friend for some time. The past six months she has cancelled plans repeatedly without a credible excuse. Although you have been friends and had the same values all along—and your mothers were childhood friends—

lately there is the sense that this friend has moved on. She has social aspirations and you realize she has become a materialistic person. In truth, she always was and you have overlooked it. Today, with her husband and children she has moved to a nearby suburb. Her friendships there are transactional—based on what someone can provide for her. No longer does time that you once shared—a shopping spree, a weekend getaway, dinner out—seem important. Her way of dealing with this is to be detached. What is most painful is that she will bow out of last minute dates with excuses that aren't credible.

Once she said she had a school conference for her twelve-year-old and you ran into her with two of her new friends. The idea that this friend would lie is disturbing, yet you've decided not to call her out. It has become obvious she would rather be with people she feels are important, even useful. Based on her texts about her calendar, there is no time left for you.

The final straw was when this friend announced she couldn't come to your son's middle school graduation party. You confronted her and she feigned nothing was wrong. That she simply had a conflict and sent an expensive gift. As if you can be bought when you were once so close. This superficial gesture has actually made you feel worse.

Today you and this friend are hardly in touch but have not severed the tie. You are the one who experiences a void. It makes you wonder what future there is for the two of you as friends.

Fracturing

Who hasn't had a close friend withdraw while we still are emotionally involved in the relationship? Often, as in the above composite, choices shift for one friend and that creates a wedge. It makes sense that the one who is left behind suffers.

Women describe feeling empty when the circumstances that united the friendship are altered. For the friend who is moving on there may be little or no upset, and this disparity makes it complicated. It also causes a power play. The friend who is disengaging and onto other experiences has made her choice, no matter how she handles it. While it might be awkward, common reactions include avoiding the friend or postponing plans.

As a result, the friendship teeters. Women of all ages in my study report that new priorities—including a love interest or work schedule or family requests and lifestyle choices—are frequently named as the reason for the rift. In later chapters we'll explore major deal breakers that are more obvious, for example a friend who steals her friend's job or concept at work, a romantic partner or another best friend. The interviewees in this chapter are dealing with an instability that seeps into their friendships. They are in agony over the beginning of the end. A difficult aspect of a friend slipping away is how it plays out. Because as females we historically have not had the voice or courage to make a clean break, the jilted friend is left in the lurch. For the friend who detaches, she leaves behind a friend who is baffled and hurt by the result.

Georg Simmel, the sociologist, believed that for pairs of friends there is an equal dependency. When one of the female friends moves on, often by partnering or by finding a new experience, the dynamics are no longer the same between them. Once their commonalities are not similar or shared, it can limit or reposition the relationship. As Rebecca Traister reminds us in her essay "What Women Find in Friends That They May Not Get From Love," "divides can creep in between friends just as easily as they do in marriages."

As evidenced below, a **faithless friend** is one who initially represented a safe haven, a friend we could count on who fit into the center of our lives. In the narratives to follow there is the view of the friend pushed aside and the view of the friend who distanced herself from the relationship. Notably, the friend who is sidelined feels deceived and saddened—we've all endured this at some point in our lives.

"The entire concept of someone not wanting to be your friend anymore cannot be simplified or generalized," Seth Shulman, a therapist who practices in Southern California, tells us. "We cannot box in how it played out or ended. The recovery is an ongoing process that often makes us question ourselves, no matter what happened."

Consider the following situations:

Shunned

> Fifteen years ago, one of my closest friends and I co-hosted a Sunday brunch for mutual friends. It went very smoothly and then she avoided me. She was living in another state and I thought doing this meal together meant something. She stayed with me, we had a great time. After that I texted and called and she barely got back to me. I wondered what I had done. One of our shared friends said she had begun an entirely different life two hundred miles away. To this day I feel I've lost out.
>
> ELLA, 47, A PARALEGAL
> LIVING IN MEMPHIS, TENNESSEE

I heard I wasn't invited to my friend's wedding through mutual friends. It was a second wedding and I was really surprised. I am the one who fixed her up with people when her husband walked out. I'm the one who tried to make her happy when she was so down and out.
The weekend of her wedding was very hard for me. That's when I realized she didn't want to be my friend. I had to face that. I'm not sure what I did, or if I did nothing at all, but she excluded me.

SORREL, 33, A PUBLICIST IN ST. PETERSBURG, FLORIDA

Set Free

Janie and I have been best friends since we were kids. Our mothers had been best friends so everything we did was a foursome growing up. When Janie went to medical school while I was trying to figure out my career, things changed. I was married first and it was like I won that round, but it came between us. Today we have little in common and I honestly don't need to be in touch. I feel pressured to see her so I do but as little as I can. We get to leave old boyfriends, don't we?

LAILA, 40, A FINANCIAL PLANNER, RELOCATING TO NORTH CAROLINA

I didn't speak to my best friend for thirty years over a man. I was dating him but he was interested in her. I was very hurt and completely shut down. It wasn't about the man but about what she had done. I stopped the

> friendship, at the time I had to let it go. I look back and realize this friend did not deserve what I did. Recently she found me on Linkedin and reached out. We live in different countries and I had chosen to be apart from her. But whatever had happened, I knew we could be friends again, on another level, without men involved.
>
> NATALIE, 56, SINGLE, IN GOVERNMENT,
> ORIGINALLY FROM MUNICH, LIVING IN OHIO

Fictive Family

When I think about what happened in my friendship with Paulette, I realize how much I wanted her to be a sister substitute for me. It filled a void, it gave our friendship an extra gloss. Women talk about it a lot, how a best friend that is like a sister means nothing could be closer or more honored. At least when it comes to rewarding sister bonds. For this reason, I'll include a few actual sister tales, where their relationship is in jeopardy and there is strife and drama, much like the friendship dyads in this book.

The attraction of a fictive family is that friends provide what is missing in our families of origin. A close friend can offer the deep connections that we long for and are missing in our families. A different kind of family—based on mutual esteem, interests, and aspirations, not blood ties or through marriage—becomes a family of choice. Think Jane Fonda and Lily Tomlin, acclaimed actresses who are friends both on and off screen. They've worked together for decades, from their 1980s film *9 to 5* to their recent work that defies ageism against women, *Grace and Frankie* (2015 to 2022), to *80 for Brady,* and *Moving On*.

Then there's *Sex and the City* where from 1998 to 2004 four single women, played by Sarah Jessica Parker, Kim Cattrall, Cynthia Nixon and Kristen Davis, support and buoy one another. There is no family to speak of (except when Miranda's character deals with her mother-in-law) and so the four friends are stand-ins for a family unit. In the 2021 version of the series, *And Just Like That*, three of the four friends, decades older and having weathered the ups and downs of life, remain each other's stalwarts. Yet Kim Cattrall's character, Samantha, is notably absent, the story line is that her character had moved to England, In June 2022, *Entertainment Weekly* quoted Sarah Jessica Parker, "It's so painful for people to keep talking about this 'catfight.' I've never uttered fighting words in my life about anybody that I've worked with ever." In June 2023, it was reported Kim Cattrall would have a cameo on the second season. Beyond this, the theme throughout the spinoff series echoes *Sex and the City*. Friends provide protection and understanding in a 'friends as family' mode.

For real life women as well, a fictive family is gratifying and a self-selected 'togetherness' that works as opposed to being assigned one's family. We hope these friends can be substitutes for our family, often for a sister, who is detached or estranged, and this creates very high expectations.

The Let Down

But even a fictive family can disappoint us. A fraught 'fictive sister' twosome has the markings of a faithless friend dyad.

As Giselle, 37, in advertising, living in Texas, reports her devastation, she and her best friend/fictive sister were torn apart by the demands of life:

My whole life my best friend was like a sister. I was married first and once that happened, I couldn't do what I usually did with her. She didn't understand how my time had changed and having a baby changed it more. Then this friend married, had two children and got divorced. Before her divorce, there was this period when we were both married and had little children. I thought we were on the same page, we'd be fine. What is crazy is that during that time she still wanted too much of my attention. She didn't think my husband needed it—she understood the kids did. She is someone who wanted a lot of energy from me and I didn't have it to spare. For years what we had in common, our race and the way we were raised, worked. Later, there were too many other things, obligations that went beyond that. She wanted us to be family to each other when we both had young families 24/7.

I apologized for my reality, hoping she'd come to accept my life, if not her own. So maybe we could come back together and resolve our differences. At the moment we're in separate places.

In contrast is Lindy, 53, an attorney living in the twin cities with three teenage sons. Her best friend since law school doesn't appreciate her efforts to make her part of the family:

I have never wanted to let this friend down. We were both far from home when we met and gave each other such support. We purposely moved to the same city and both of us work at big firms. Since my boys were little, I included my friend in whatever we did together. She decided not to be married, not to have children. Those were her choices. She is an aunt, a godmother to my boys.

She has filled in for me for their school events and has been there for me. I've been there too—I am her family and she is part of ours.

When she first pulled away, I was traumatized. I still think about it every day. She stopped spending time with my kids, after she saw the mothers who help each other and help me out—football moms and soccer moms. She assumed I didn't need her, she thought it was a way of pushing her out. Why not think how good it is for me to have this lineup of mothers for carpooling and sports? That she didn't understand makes me feel drained. I wish someone could tell me how this can be better, why it happened. I am very sad and sorry. It causes anxiety.

Eighty percent of the women in this study believe their closest female friends are able to save them from anxious moments. It's a tall order yet throughout this book women describe looking to their female friends for a safe haven and often over amplify what a friend can do. According to psychologist Abraham Maslow's famed "Hierarchy of Needs," the category of love/belonging encompasses friendship and family and sexual intimacy. This is placed in the middle of his five-point pyramid. The need for friendship and family is situated above physiological needs (ranked the lowest and most basic), then safety needs (ranked second from the bottom). Friendship and family and love interests are situated below self-esteem (ranked number four) and the final need, which is self-actualization (ranked number five). The third level is critical because it is after we have each cared for ourselves physically (physiological then safety) that we aspire for intimacy with friends and our families. This underscores how much we value our friendships and how devastating it can be when the relationship goes awry.

The Bar Too High

Consider Scarlett, a 65-year-old who does freelance editing and lives in Palm Springs, California. Presently single, she has no children and has been married three times:

> About eight years ago a friend and I worked together at a restaurant. We had become very close but our lives were not similar. We were from different backgrounds, she was European and I am American born and bred. I had been attempting a career in acting and I worked at this restaurant to keep afloat. She was happily married with an extended family and in a good place. I was between husbands and on my own. I saw from the start what an entitled person she was. She had this attitude that she was gracing me with her presence. She was very good looking and so she got her way with staff and her clients at the restaurant. I'd say it was like we were related, where you are not the same type but totally connected.
>
> What triggered us was one event at the restaurant. It was a holiday that meant a lot to me. She had said she wasn't going to work that day and so I had to. She knew it was the only day of the year that mattered to me but if she wanted it off, I'd work. I thought it was the right thing to do. We looked out for each other. Then she came in and I was extremely upset. I could have taken the day off. She was aware of how I felt.
>
> Afterward, I was so angry at the manager and at my friend. I felt betrayed. We had spoken about traveling together and putting money away to make it happen. I decided against it and I told her. For a long while we still

were together at the restaurant but it wasn't easy, we were falling apart. I knew I had to move on. Who knows what she expected or wanted.

Provocations

Scarlett's narrative punctuates how one episode forces us to face what's lacking in an important friendship. First there is a dramatic action followed by the two friends' reaction and then outcome. What becomes apparent is that the shared intimacy and caring has diminished, in some instances evaporated. The upset friend has to face this reality. Possibly her friend isn't conscious of what has occurred. The truth is, she isn't into the friendship anymore, and so the outcome doesn't matter as much to her. When it becomes evident that a relationship that means a lot to us no longer means a lot to our friend, how do we bounce back? How do we move forward?

Melissa, 33, working in retail in San Diego, is married with two young children. She was devastated when her friend failed her in her darkest hour:

> I have had this friend since our twenties. We are from the same background and were raised similarly. It was a positive experience at the start. She was my best friend for years until there was tension, something I can't explain. That was what first changed our friendship.
>
> Then I had a child who died at three years old. I expected this friend to do everything a close friend would do. It was what I wanted her to do, to be there for me and she wasn't. I began to question our friendship, we had some words and then we didn't speak for six months.

Our husbands were asking for us to get back together, they wanted us to talk about this issue. We are trying to solve what happened. She and I do not have common friends. She is the friend who meant everything to me. I began questioning what I asked of her. Like I'm pouring from a cup and she was not pouring back. That I put more into this friendship than she did. I considered leaving because I wasn't getting what I needed. I talked to my friends and family. Someone said maybe she'll come back in other ways as a friend. But she didn't come through with my child. That was a big loss. I am still bitter in my heart over what she did.

I can't think of making other friends, someone who comes through in both happy times and sad times. I had needed this friend to be with me, to lean on.

Researching and interviewing for *Estranged*, I was struck by how many of us don't really know the person we peg a 'trusted friend' until a time of great joy or great sorrow. At the critical hour, it is surprising who is there for us and who is not. Roberta Satow, in her essay in *Psychology Today*, "How Friendships Evolve Throughout the Lifecycle," defines high stakes friendships versus low stakes friendships. With a high stakes friend, there is a true bond, the friends share innermost feelings and depend on one another during trying situations. With a low stakes friend, the emotions are not on the same level and personal feelings are not shared. Instead it is a more superficial connection. In Melissa's high stakes friendship, the 'inciting incident' was a tragic personal event in her life. The question becomes, what can she hope to receive going forward after she has witnessed her friend's inability to give during a crisis.

For Colleen, 35, a program manager in San Francisco, married with no children, a series of failures triggered the teetering of a valued friendship. While hers was not a tragic event, she echoes Melissa when she considers the price of new friendships:

> We were best friends for over fifteen years. We had the kind of friendship where we could talk about everything, there were no barriers. We'd lived in the same town growing up and after college moved to different parts of the country. This friend has never been married. We didn't compete with one another. She was one of the top five people in my life, including family.
>
> One of the first cracks in our friendship came about when we were younger and went clubbing. I had to leave early, and she felt abandoned but didn't say it. There was no confrontation because she couldn't voice her disappointment. Then we talked about traveling together, and that didn't work out. There was nothing I could do to fix it, to make up for it. Next she moved to Chicago without really telling me her plans. Each of these sounds like a minor incident but when we add it together, it is one big disappointment. I hung onto the friendship. I kept trying to build it back up. She said she was disappointed and didn't tell me what I could do to help.
>
> My marriage caused a wedge, it didn't work out when my friend and I were together with my husband. My life is very different since she and I are not in touch. It is an emptiness, this friendship grounded me. I think her insecurities are what ruined our friendship. She became distant. It was how she could manage what had changed between us.

Similarly to Colleen, Jackie, 46, a working mother with two teenage children, living in Detroit, believes too much came between her and her best friend:

> This friend didn't understand my obligations. I have a husband, kids, an elderly mother and a job as a supervisor at a big box store. This friend, who I adored, couldn't accept it. There was a time when I had to break plans. It was for a ski weekend and I thought my kids were covered, that my sister-in-law would take care of them. When that fell apart, my friend didn't get it. Then she just sort of slipped away and I felt unbound.
>
> I tried to replace this sense of community with other, new friends. I am looking for a network now because there was too much emphasis placed on this one friend. I'm not sure I could start this kind of bond with one person after this failed. We texted and emailed for years. When I think of her now, it hurts. I've not fully recovered from what went wrong.
>
> She was the needier friend and I didn't' realize it. I didn't understand her as well as I thought I did. She seemed to believe my commitments meant I didn't care about her and about the friendship, and it wasn't true.

For women, giving up female friends for the sake of their marriages can prove precarious. Behavioral scientist Paul Dolan has been quoted saying "If you're a man, you should probably get married. If you're a woman, don't bother." This is based on his research findings that long-term social bonds such as empathetic listening, gratitude, forgiveness, are not always cultivated in a marriage. Yet these traits are meant to be found among our closest female friends.

Concessions

Erich Fromm noted in his book, *The Art of Loving,* that humans feel an "existential loneliness." If we apply this feeling to our female friendships, we realize it is a part of the problem. What better way to combat this than with a coterie of friends? *The Harvard Business Review* published a study showing that women with solid friendships are headed for higher pay and more executive placement. This should bode well for strong female friendships, but if the center does not hold the result is anything but strengthening.

When a friendship begins to falter, some women choose to reframe it. They will remain in touch or, alternatively, take a break from the level of contact. Several interviewees report how complicated this decision can be and how much uncertainty and conflict it renders.

Brier, 35, from Cleveland, where she writes ads and is single, describes her struggles with her best friend as ongoing:

> I live with three female friends including my best friend. I am still with her but not sure how to fix things. We've known each other since elementary school. There has been a negative toll with this friend since we were kids. I have always been her friend though, and to this day, I check in with her. She talks about herself constantly, while being distracted by her phone or she'll talk only about herself. The conversations are very one-sided. She doesn't listen to me, always it's her needs, and her life. She doesn't ask about me. So it's like she's not there but sitting with me, thinking about herself. Because we're like family, if I ended this friendship, she would fall into a depression. Others have left her and I know it wouldn't

be right to do that. We've even been sick together, and in a strange way, after all that she does, I know she is a comfort to me. I can be myself with her, and if I can get her to listen, I am able to flag down her support.

So when I doubt myself or realize how she isn't a productive or well person, I know I can't leave her. There have been instances where we've had to stand up for each other. But now I wonder if something goes wrong, would she stand up for me? And I doubt it. I'm not sure I want to stay friends. I've tried to push my needs forward somehow, but she is always first. If I tell her how I feel, she doesn't hear it.

Nan, 48, who works in a bakery in Tulsa, Oklahoma, has been loyal to a fault to a best friend who lives next door:

I definitely have other friends where it is easier and when I compare them to her, they are refreshing. I realize what a joyful friendship is because of my other friends, but this friend is single and has no children. We go back so far, we have this history of being close even when there have been problems, when she is stable. My home is hers. There have been great times in the past. I don't want to hurt her or upset her. Sometimes I think I'd miss her terribly if we were apart. I have never known a life without her. We get together a few times a month and speak daily. On the other hand, she is hurting me and our friendship brings me down. She is short tempered and too sensitive so I don't like spending time and I find it upsetting.

I am not sure that my friend knows how I feel about her and it's gotten worse in the past few years. I am no

longer sure what to do. I want to express what I need
or else we can't keep being friends. Do I stay out of fear
of hurting her when in reality I'm just hurting myself?
I wrestle back and forth with this.

Glenda, 39, an administrator who lives in northern New Jersey, was crushed when her close friend, wanted a 'fancy husband' and decided Glenda no longer fit in with her plans:

It worked while we were in school—being from the same
background—then she started putting me down. She said
I wore corny clothes and I was too sensitive. Basically she
dumped me because she had this crazy plan to find a rich,
fancy husband. I didn't fit in and she wasn't going to let
anything get in her way. But what bothered me so much
was that I didn't see it coming and didn't know she was
like that. Maybe it would have been better if we never
saw one another again. Instead I was put into another
category for her very specific plan.

Rudderless

Sometimes, our expectations can create a zero-sum game: if one person wins, the other loses. If it were a family drama, we might make an excuse and find a way to go forward. If it were a romantic relationship, there might be conversations, even rules and guides for how to hammer it out. Yet with friends who are on the brink, with one friend clinging to what was and the other about to turn away, there is confusion and a sense of desertion.

In novels, we witness the ups and downs of these bonds.

Firefly Lane by Kristin Hannah, follows Tully and Kate, best friends since childhood, who endure rifts and jealousies as their friendship falls to ruin. Dana Spiotta's novel, *Innocents and Others,* is about two women who are filmmakers, Meadow Mori, who makes intellectual films and Carrie Wexler, who creates commercial work. They vary in how they treat each other, from being unkind to truly caring. As Lillian Rubin in her book, *Just Friends,* reminds us, "With no social compact, no ritual moment, no pledge of loyalty and constancy to hold a friendship in place, it becomes not only the most neglected social relationship of our time, but all too often, our most fragile one as well."

It isn't because we don't feel deeply that our female friendship might end up short on commitment compared to our marriage or the bond to our children. It is more likely that there is no model for these relationships once they become complicated. Clearly, as stated above, all the feelings are in place without a resolution. Nonetheless, these friendships are held to a high scrutiny, making them vulnerable to conflict and injury. In enough cases, homophily—where we form social connections with those who are our gender, age, level of education and income and share our personal beliefs—has a strong appeal. This provides a safe haven, we are known to each other, many times since childhood or our school days.

As I wrap up this chapter, I remember a commuter friend from long ago who was so important to me. We had a lot in common; we talked books, family, in-laws, swimming. There was a sense of camaraderie followed by a vanishing act on her part. When I moved out of town and tried to stay in touch, she could never find time on her calendar for us to meet at a halfway point. This raised questions and I was forced to face myself. Had I been the one who sought her out? Was I imagining she cared as much as I did? Had I ever treated a friend as she treated me?

If we soul search, we realize the consequences of a faithless friend, having been one or endured one at some juncture in our lives.

Do you have a Faithless Friend or are you one? Here are some questions to consider:

Do you believe that your expectations are too high?

Friendships shapeshift with time and circumstances. If you cannot adjust and be flexible, you might be contributing to the friction between you and your friend.

Are you able to face that this important friendship is now in limbo?

Women devastated by the pivot of a treasured friendship need to look closely at their assumptions. What was once at the center of the friendship might no longer hold up. If you are moving in different directions for example, your friend might be pulling back.

Why are you holding onto a friend who is not interested in you anymore?

We fantasize about a perfect best friendship much as we do about a perfect partner. This sentiment contributes to why we cling when the friendship is waning and our friend is not giving back.

Do you believe this friendship can be placed in a less central part of your life?

Once you choose to detach, you are putting the friendship in jeopardy. The question becomes how messy this will be and whether things can be reconfigured.

What steps will you take to move away from the friend?

A woman who instigates the 'distancing' often views the faithless friend as the problem. This justifies her actions. She is certain that she and her friend do not belong together anymore.

SHE SAID / SHE SAID

EXHIBIT A: **The Sacrifice**

Maggie and Anne

For this section, I've been able to interview both sides of a friendship narrative. In this dyad, we'll begin with Maggie, 49, who regrets how Anne became "a faithless friend." For both women, the disappointment of a friendship being pushed aside for the sake of a man has caused lasting wounds.

Maggie

> The last time I'd seen Anne was at that dinner at my apartment. After that she disappeared. I couldn't register the loss.

•

> Over twenty years ago, when I was first married, I invited one of my closest friends, Anne, over for dinner. I thought it was a perfect evening and then poof, she was gone from my life. I tried to reach her—I kept trying. Finally, I got the distinct impression that she didn't want to be in touch. I couldn't understand why. I assumed that I'd done something wrong and that she was no longer interested which was painful. Except this was Anne. We had been bonded through our summers together, we did exciting things and shared so much. It couldn't be that she was missing.

For Maggie, when Anne vanished it brought back memories of other college friends she had lost. She began to distrust herself, old fears resurfaced. Was she not hip enough, was it uncool to be a wife?

> I didn't have a very large wedding, only sixty people and it mattered that my friends were there. I remember that Anne wanted to make a toast and what she said was very heartfelt. That's how close we were.

Belonging

Today, Maggie, 50, is a yoga teacher and lives in New Orleans. She was married for twelve years and has no children. Without any siblings, friendships have been a critical part of her life. Maggie had met Anne her freshman year of college when they were living in the same dorm. Maggie, who was quiet and shy, noticed gregarious, extroverted Anne right away. Maggie's family, after living overseas, had settled in the same Delaware area where Anne's family lived, a connection that brought them closer. As opposites, the two gravitated toward each other:

> She knew about film and recommended offbeat movies. We'd go hear a band play and it felt like we were equals. But she had this knowledge about things—how did she know? By our senior year in college Anne had a serious boyfriend. That was something we all wanted. She didn't seem to be doing much schoolwork. She had a more relaxed approach and was pulled along by her own ideas.

Maggie felt 'irked' and at the same time envious of Anne's casual attitude toward life. What created another layer of cool, as Maggie viewed it, was how liberal Anne's parents were while her own parents were more conservative. Maggie imagined Anne's family sitting around the dinner table discussing philosophers and artists while her own talked about television shows. All of this contributed to what Maggie saw as Anne's level of confidence. Maggie had no family experiences that were sophisticated or unconventional.

When they were students, Maggie had several friendship breakups. She and Anne and another friend were very close, until the other friend "drifted away." Another friend was furious when Maggie told her that her boyfriend was unfaithful and she "broke up" with Maggie. These incidents shattered Maggie's trust in friends while her connection to Anne remained solid throughout.

Men as Friendship Busters

Maggie was married at 29 and segued from single life to young married mode, sharing time with other newlyweds. Anne wasn't part of the picture. Thus she had never met Anne's boyfriend who became her husband. Nor was she invited to Anne's wedding. Not being included only added to the pain of Anne's disappearance. The consequences of being without Anne lasted for years and she missed her.

Recently, as the years have gone on and her parents have gotten older, Maggie has begun to think of friends as family. She realized she needed to better understand what kind of female friendships would work for her:

> I thought about the friends I'd lost touch with and the good parts with everyone from Anne to this recent friendship that was over. What these women at different stages had brought into my life. But through it all, being iced and icing, I've asked myself, am I one of these people who cuts a friend off and had I done it for a male partner? And what it is that triggers me. I began to wonder if with these lost friendships, I was looking for too much. Sometimes I think I need to analyze myself to understand what's gone on, what did I do or not do. It is what I haven't talked about with my friends that troubles me the most.

Rediscovery

At this juncture she considered lost friends of her past and decided to search for Anne on social media:

> I was hoping to find her. I so wanted to know how she was. I went on Facebook and learned Anne was alive and well. There had been almost nineteen years of not seeing her. Again, the questions—how did she and I ever fall apart? More than that, I was just so happy to know we could reach out. Until then I had this false idea that it was my fault alone. Now there was a second chance.

When Anne contacted Maggie in the summer of 2019, Maggie was driving through the Pacific Northwest, an hour away from where Anne lives. Maggie received an Instant Message and believed it was "meant to be." She and her travel companion drove directly to see Anne:

> I didn't want to rehash our history. We didn't discuss the past because we had limited time. It didn't seem appropriate so we focused on the positive. I was afraid to push it after there had been other losses with my friends.
> We have the same politics, which matters these days. I realize how divided people are now and it's the first time I've only wanted to be with someone who sees situations as I do. One of my college friends ghosted me recently because we don't see eye to eye on politics. Today, there's no way I could be with someone who doesn't have my views. I was relieved to find out that Anne and I were in synch, that we wouldn't have a problem with who we voted for. But what counts most is that we are friends again.

Maggie's cultivated self-awareness dovetails with her high hopes for a revitalized friendship with Anne:

> I'm confident that Anne and I will be in touch from now on. We're both active on social media and even with our busy lives, we can connect. My takeaway is, if you want to get in touch with an old friend, there is no reason to not try. I thought throughout the years that Anne had made a conscious decision to break up with me, to take me out of her life. We don't dwell on lost years and since we hadn't anticipated finding each other again, being reunited is remarkable.

Anne

> Once I took up with Dan, the energy I had for friendships went to his circle rather than to mine. That included Maggie.
>
> •
>
> I had all these friends and there I was withdrawing. I was 34 years old and had just gotten married, I was supposed to be married. Drifting away from my closest women friends included Maggie. I told myself things had shifted with our lifestyles. She was married earlier. But what really happened was that leaving her was part of my pattern, it was who I had become.

Losing Out to a Spouse

Today, Anne, 49, is divorced without children and lives in the Pacific Northwest. In retrospect she realizes she let her important female friendships slide when she married and her husband, an outsider, became the wedge. She easily moved into wife mode, leaving Maggie behind in the process. As someone who made friends easily throughout her life, Anne viewed these bonds as meaningful. She described herself as seeking stability in her college friendships and viewing Maggie as one of her early, essential friends:

> At school in Philadelphia, I was friends with everyone. I wasn't competitive about anything, I was only an okay student, but I had friends from every social sphere. Maggie and I were from middle class families and the same religion. Our parents stayed married because this was the practice. Maggie and I shared so much, there was a mutual caring.
>
> Right after school, most of us stayed in the city and ended up living there and were extremely close. For me it was an intermittent continuation of college, like dorm life that had mattered so much. These friends became my circle. Maggie and her friends weren't a part of it.

Excluding Not Including

After all Anne's energy and care went into these female bonds, she readily unloaded those valuable ties for her husband. Yet she knew deep down it wasn't the right choice. Worse, it reminded her of her mother's style and Anne knew that it hadn't been a good decision. By ignoring these warning signs and choosing to give all her attention and energy to her husband and marriage, her friendships suffered from tension and then loss.

The level of damage to Anne's historic friendships and her personal style of being a friend wasn't apparent until afterward:

For the nine years I spent with Dan, we never discussed my friends, including Maggie, in any detail. It was surreal how while we were a team and loved each other, I was asleep and in denial about the entire thing. Like this was the path, the natural progression. We had no discussions about the life I cared about. I'd simply gone along with it. I was letting friends go. I allowed Dan a lot of control. My friends had never controlled me, which is maybe why I could leave. I look back at how I missed them without understanding how this was happening.

Repairing

When she and Maggie found each other on Facebook, Anne was thrilled to be in touch again. Maggie's road trip to the Pacific Northwest placed their reunion in real time. Anne, grateful for the chance to reconnect, saw it as a second chance. For a long while she had been struggling with the sense she'd made "a mess of things."

> I have learned to have more compassion for myself when it comes to my friends, my family and my marriage. Maggie and I are on opposite sides of the country but there are ways to stay connected and when we do, we are really close. We are similar to when we were in college. It feels like we picked up where we left off, it's comfortable and familiar. We share a history and have common viewpoints in extremely troubling times.
>
> That would include our politics. Politics have been a big part of my life and while I try to be kind and honest in listening to both sides, when it comes to policies or lifestyle I have a certain viewpoint. I try to be open

and honest and I believe that friends need to be able to talk about it. Some people think differently than I do. But I cannot be truly close to someone who has opposite beliefs, not today, not with how the world is. This is how things have changed. Maggie and I agree on our worldview. To be honest, it's a relief because we've missed blocks of time with one another over so many years.

I am still trying to understand what my role in this friendship is, how to be a better friend. I have always valued Maggie's humor and openness, that she's a listener and has compassion.

Unexpected Priorities

With their distinctive styles, both Maggie and Anne had been drawn into the same formula whereby one's marriage dictates her friendship selection. What is more surprising is how Anne, an independent spirit and leader among her friends, was influenced once she was partnered, then married.

In the Maggie/Anne fall-out of almost twenty years, there was no conversation, no confrontation, rather a benign silence. While women are known to avoid conflict, according to the National Alternative Dispute Resolution Advisory Council, they also show empathy and respect when asked to resolve disputes. That brings us to what an open communication can yield. While for practically two decades Maggie blamed herself and questioned what happened to her friendship with Anne, Anne was going through seismic shifts in her own identity. Yet the two friends had not spoken or shared their feelings and had become estranged. They lost the time together and the chance to understand the other's circumstances.

Can This Friendship Be Saved?

Two marriages that sabotaged a friendship remind us how often women stratify their relationships. Both Maggie and Anne allowed a commitment to a romantic partner to come between them. Their emotional connection was forfeited and their marriages overshadowed the connection the two friends shared.

Delighted as Maggie and Anne are to be reunited—with a keen awareness that few of us get a second chance at a long-lost friendship—there is caution surrounding their present interactions. The feelings are in place, having never dissipated, but there is also a history of losing each other.

What is key today is for both women to respect the restored relationship while mindful of their past mistakes. For each of us in terms of our female friends, there is the need to be self-aware and transparent. In so doing we preserve the good in our meaningful friendships, renegotiating if need be and we admit what is not authentic and cannot be salvaged.

CHAPTER TWO

A Wayward Friend

Do you have a close friend who engages in unsound behavior?

Are you constantly uneasy about the friend?

Is there a secret but you know about it?

Have you asked her to stop and to seek help?

Is there a path out for her and do you feel responsible?

If you have checked any yeses to the above, you have a friend who is in jeopardy, physically or emotionally or financially—or in combination:

> It isn't your first rodeo with your dear friend of the past sixteen years. Who knows why you were seduced by her from the start. You met in your mid-thirties at a Pilates class and began spending time together in purposeful ways; lectures, birdwatching, film and theatre. At first you didn't notice she liked to drink and once you did, it still took another year to understand she drank no matter

what the occasion and at inappropriate times. Who needs a drink before an afternoon at a spa in Florida? Why, in fact, did she drink on the morning flight to Florida?

But she is so charming, smart, attractive and social, you must be wrong to doubt her. Your feeling that she dabbles in a drink too many might be judgmental. Who are you to do that? Besides, over the years, her drinking hasn't increased and her patterns have remained the same. Whenever you are on the brink of reaching out to her mother or sister, she shows up looking radiant and fresh and she's high functioning at work. Aren't you wrong to doubt her?

A year ago her husband called to say this friend had crashed their new SUV into the garage door. She had been at a cousin's wedding shower and had too much to drink. Yet it wasn't an isolated incident, he said, rather that the only time she didn't drink too much and pop pills only in moderation, was with you. Pop pills? you asked. Are you certain—he was very certain. The family wanted to know if you could help with an intervention. Since there have been nagging doubts about your friend and you have been passive, telling yourself it can't be so, you know it is time to be on board. They are fortunate that they can afford inpatient treatment. Your friend comes back after three months renewed, refreshed and sober. She has joined AA and you have joined the support group for family members and friends. It's all promising but you are still uneasy.

Within two weeks of her return, the two of you go to Bloomingdales. That's when you realize she has a new addiction. She is a shopaholic now while in recovery for being an alcoholic. When she charges four thousand dollars on her credit card in less than an hour, you wonder how to stop this. Should you rat her out, call her husband at work tomorrow? Can you finally stop rationalizing her behaviors?

Flash Warnings

In the composite above, our narrator describes her hesitancy and a 'late to the game' responsibility for a friend who has had a drinking problem for years. Her rationale being that it was always within her friend's control. Fifty percent of the women interviewed for this chapter report that they know whatever secret their friend is hiding. While above it's about alcoholism, recovery and then a newfound shopping addiction that substitutes for the drinking, other inappropriate conducts affect women.

The closest friendships are stricken by such a heavy burden. Whatever time they share, the friend who is engaged in these behaviors is complicating life for her friend. Even if the bystanding friend talks herself out of it, she knows her friend needs help. Still, looking the other way—a form of wishful thinking—is easier. We know this.

Having witnessed how an outside force disrupts a closely-knit pair of friends in Chapter One, a **wayward friend** is a different type of challenge. The threat to the friendship stems from dangerous behavior and poor judgment of one of the two friends. For the friend who is under an influence—it could be addiction (substance abuse, gambling, shopping), a pattern of lying, anorexia, unsavory love interests, or poor financial decisions—there is the constant threat of being discovered. A friendship that is loaded down by the person *and* her issue, is filled with turmoil. The tension intensifies when the wayward friend is in the throes of her issue and instability threatens the dyad.

On the flip side is the devoted friend who hopes to help her troubled friend but the situation is often too serious. This takes a toll on both women.

Consider Natasha, 39, a stay-at-home mother of two, living in the Southwest:

> No one else can get near this friendship, we are that close. But we have terrible fights because she can't stay sober. She has lost jobs and two husbands because of her drinking and drugging. I used to cover for her but she makes the worst choices and the cleanup is becoming too heavy for me. I have my family to think of too. When she's not high, she agrees with me. When she's using, it is scary. Like she's two different people. We have been together since we were in pre-school. How can I turn my back on her now?

Similarly to Natasha is Reese, 46, who feels she has 'fronted' for her best friend. Reese works in fashion, is married and has a teenage son. The family lives in Maryland.

> How would I trust myself to have the right friendship after what I've been through with this friend? She has stayed with me for months at a time and I've had to lie to my husband about her. She is an online gambler and spends hours at it, losing to the point I've even given her money. Being her support system is lonely, there's no one left in her family or among her friends who would still cover for her. It won't end, she's my friend.

Blind Devotion

According to the American Addiction Centers, the behavioral signs of an addiction include anxiety, agitation, lack of motivation, loss of interest, and withdrawal from friends and family. For the friend in a twosome who is not addicted, she is aware of the symptoms but remains fiercely loyal.

In Karen Young's article, "When Someone You Love Has an Addiction," she describes how profound a path it is for an addict to self-destruction. She warns there is nothing we as a friend or as family can do and advises us to question what we get from the relationship. And as we have realized in this chapter, for some interviewees, there is no choice but to leave the friendship for the sake of self-preservation. While for others, there is a commitment to the long haul.

That being said, poor habits get in the way of how exceptional the friendship can be. Marilyn Monroe's drug and alcohol use affected her close friendship with Ella Fitzgerald, according to Sara Kettler in Biography.com.In Robyn Crawford's personal book, *A Song for You: My Life with Whitney Houston,* Houston's drug use was a part of their friendship of many years. The National Library of Medicine reports that if there is Alcohol Use Disorder (AUD) in a marriage, the rates of dissolution are at 48.3% and if there is no AUD, the rate is at 30.1%. When I researched rates in a long-standing female friendships, I wasn't able to locate statistics. However, the National Library of Medicine notes how women recovering from a substance use feel about female bonds. These women say their reconnection to other women offers a sense of power and positivity. This finding reminds us that if the friend does not go into recovery, there is a tremendous toll on the friendship. Over seventy percent of my interviewees said they are not confident they can stay with a friend immersed in drug and/or alcohol use. Ninety percent claimed the relationship, despite a true connection, is harmed by the situation.

Rule Breakers

For the rule breaker, whatever her motivation (this not only applies to addiction), her friend tolerates the effect and is unhappy. Women report the frustration of being with a friend engaged in extreme behavior. For example, this friend may chronically lie, often to justify her choices (as opposed to Chapter Five where women construct one specific whopper). What about a friend who is unstable when it comes to relationships, work, children or those whose decisions are driven by money? Women with friends entrenched in these actions admit the friendships are taxed. As for the friend who is wayward, she either grapples to get on safe ground or she is too entrenched to bother. The salient question being, what are we, as the friends at the receiving end, left to do?

Secrets

Intimacy and self-disclosure matter greatly to women. Collins and Miller's study, *Self-Disclosure and Liking,* found that the more we disclose the more well liked we are. Dindia and Allen report in their research, *Sex Differences in Self-disclosure,* that women win at revealing themselves while men reveal less. That's why when it comes to the wayward friend, we still expect the whole story. That's why when a friend lies by omission, we're rattled. How about for the friend covering up, how is it for her?

Consider Rose, 52, an administrator who lives in Ft. Lauderdale and has one child:

> I have always had close female friends and value them. What happened with my closet friend since we were kids is a turning point. I got caught in a lie at her big bash. Someone overheard me telling my lie and ratted me out. When I looked over at my dearest friend (we no longer speak) she knew what I had done. She was furious. This happened right before the pandemic and that made it harder to fix, it was a crazy time.
>
> The lie was silly but it hangs over me. She had asked me to bring a carload of her guests. I said there was no room in the car and that I had to drop people at my sister's place before I got to hers. I couldn't tell the truth, it was because my car was filled with my friends. I was trying to sneak them in. I assumed once she saw them there, she'd be fine. After she heard what I'd done, I thought we were okay. I didn't think it would become a war.
>
> She let our friendship go, she didn't so much as confront me, she made it into a deadlock. What I realized about it is that I never wanted her to learn the truth and I'd lied to her before. I thought I could pull it off. Now our forty-year friendship is over. She is like an aunt to my daughter and she doesn't care, she's dropped her too. The way she cut me off makes me feel like I did something worse than I did. I'm not being invited to her home, and I'm ex-communicated. All of it has been taken away, I keep thinking one day it will get better, it has to. Somehow we'll be in touch again.

Rose is remorseful but also surprised that her friend responded as she did, as if her lie was not that relevant. The other point of view, from the person who has been lied to, comes from Liese, 32, a kindergarten teacher, who describes being the recipient of a lie. She lives in Salt Lake City with her fiancé and works in retail:

> My best friend lied to me about her new position and plan to move to the northeast. When I found out through a mutual friend, but someone not as close to her as I am, she defended what she did. And she lied more, saying it wasn't for certain it would go through. Except she'd sold her house and it was obvious she was doing this. She just hadn't bothered to tell me. She has lied before about things, she has been sneaky, it's almost pathological. I stopped talking to her and seeing her as we had before and distanced myself.
>
> But she sent texts saying how awful life is without me, and then we ran into each other at a friend's one-year-old's birthday party. And our mutual friends have tried to patch things up. I decided later that I'm really angry because she treated me like I'm not important enough. I also thought of how we were very close, like sisters, more than best friends. I'm not sure I can let this friendship be over although I also know the lies won't stop. I'm not sure of the future but I'm sure of how I feel about her.

What I found curious in Liese's and Rose's narratives is how much loss both women experience. The end of Rose's friendship, although she is not repentant, is filled with sorrow. Liese is offended and hurt but not ready to let her friendship go. Both interviewees are in deep with their reactions and insistent their stance is the only way to be.

Cast Aside

From the time we are young, we know the pitfalls of threesomes, the curse of three. Whether it's a fifth-grade memory, a college experience, or a workplace effect, when there are three friends together, there is often an odd person out. Perhaps one friend is more dominating, or two out of the three friends feel closer to each other than to the third friend. Randi Mazzella writes in *How to Navigate A Friendship Threesome* that it is "not an equilateral triangle." With this awareness, in theory it should work, but it can backfire. Your friend may fall prey to a negative influence, or one friend may become close with a destructive third person, making your own friendship untenable.

Let's look at Marthe, 60, who lives in Alabama and works in personal services. She has no children:

> I have never wanted to reinvent myself, and I always had a quad squad of friends, for forty-five years. We met in our twenties and thirties and we have hung together. It is a quality circle, we get together three or four times a month. Then one friend, who I am closest to, separated from her husband. We knew the new man she was seeing wasn't right. My hunch was he wasn't really a good guy, he was a drifter. My friend had him move into her house. She had been separated for years and we'd all been so close. But this pattern changed and she stopped talking to us. She was only available when she was walking the dog. Then she decided to move to California. This man is the one influencing her. He's taken her money and she's starting to agree with him about everything. I lost my friend to her new boyfriend. I think he's a fake, something is not right. Our whole group feels this way, we aren't

fifteen anymore with a boyfriend who might come or go, who might or not be trustworthy.

My friend has done a total 180 turn. It extends to everything in her life, she has no judgment anymore. I am very depressed and sad. This man has so influenced my friend it's like he's switched her brain. She has lost herself and it is very upsetting to us. Our group all sees how she has distanced herself. I worry now that this man will screw her over in the long run. Ever since she started with him, she's lied to us, slowly, over the course of two years. She used to be so smart and now she isn't intelligent. She's dropped everyone and no one can imagine what she sees in this man. She has cleared us out of her life and moved away from us. She isn't herself anymore or she's not as smart as I thought she was.

I feel betrayed because she turned out to be such a liar about her family, her ex-husband. She is nothing like she was. If she comes back to me, if it doesn't work with this new man, I will take my time and distance myself. Who she has become has been that awful, I don't trust her anymore, I don't know who she is anymore."

Marthe's disappointment and sorrow over her best friend's almost cult-like devotion to an outsider/third wheel in the form of a new boyfriend is easy to understand. What makes it more complicated is how she observes her friend's obsession with this man and cannot be heard. She is frustrated because she has been removed from her friend's life without any ability to change the landscape. Her friend is lying for the cause and Marthe knows she can't be heard about this. Her friend's choices have caused the kind of distance that seems irreparable. Marthe is suffering the consequences.

While Marthe is deeply troubled over her friend who is no longer available and her love interest who is the cause, Noreen, 49, from Sonoma, Arizona, is the flip side of this experience. Noreen reports the decisions she has made for a man and his level of sway, which has impacted her best friendship. She has two sons and works in the food industry:

> I left my husband for another man. When I told my best friend, she was critical and said I should wake up and stop this. She said it wasn't fair to my children and that I don't seem to hear anyone but this man. I ask myself if I would look at a friend who was doing exactly what I'm doing and find fault or be concerned. After the last get together, he made some judgments about my son and that bothered me. But who can I tell? My best friend is already against this match and is warning me not to marry him.
>
> My mother died and my closest friends all came over to help me out. It was so nice and I thought, finally they'll see how this man is, they'll understand. Instead one friend called him greedy and another said he had taken over my thoughts. That love is blind. She said I should talk to his last girlfriend and learn the story, he has a pattern.
>
> The outcome of this is that I only have superficial conversations with friends who aren't supportive. I'm not going to confront my best friend. Either she's there for me, or she's not. I don't want to hear her negative thoughts about the man I'm about to marry.

Sister Revenge/Sister Loss

In adding one sister narrative here, I'd like to point out that Diandra, 60, living in Southern California where she works in textiles, and her sister Lisa, 54, living in Colorado, have not spoken in over twenty years:

> My sister and I were supposed to get along but we never really did and it was hard for my mother, not for my sister and me. We were like oil and water. We never had the same interests or taste in anything. We grew up in the same house and were exposed to all the same things but didn't feel the same. She was never a good daughter, She didn't make it easy for my parents as a teenager and in college especially. When we were together, I tried and I wanted to be close. There were times when it worked out, but mostly we were just in the same house growing up with a mother who wanted us to be true sisters. We weren't naturally drawn to each other at all.
>
> We have one younger sister who I am close with and we work together. Lisa never got involved with our family business. Our grandfather had started it, we were fabric manufacturers. As the business grew, Lisa seemed even more detached from things.
>
> I married first as the eldest and have two grown daughters. Lisa has four children but no one has seen them in years. She and her husband joined a cult of sorts and separated completely from our family. This was heartbreaking for my mother. She suffered and so did my little sister who loved us both. For Lisa it was a war against me and our family. Really it came down to money and she was vicious, it wasn't normal how she acted. She kept insisting on more money.

After all these years without my sister in my life, I'm okay. I've learned to view her realistically. Had Lisa been a good person, I'd have the relationship. Had she not been crazily angry, that would have helped. I am realistic. I have great women friends and I consider myself a reliable, respectful friend. I probably did it in reaction to my missing sister. I trust my women friends since I can't trust my sister. Even if Lisa called and came back, who can forgive her for making the rest of us so miserable? My two girls feel they don't have an aunt and my mother has missed her daughter. What good can come it?

Tricky Times

If we think of our shared histories with our friends, at some point, for enough of us, there was a friend who was unstable in some way. No matter what stage of life this occurred, there is the shock factor when someone we care about veers off on a dangerous or destructive path. Interviewees report being left dazed, wondering what to do.

In high school, I had a friend who was always in charge. Everyone fell under her spell. She encouraged her followers to gang up on other girls in the class, practically ruining them. It was a real-life *Mean Girls,* reminiscent of the Tina Fey film. Or *Cat's Eye, the* Margaret Atwood novel where the protagonist, Elaine, recalls her friend from school, Cordelia, who treated her at times brutally, at times benignly. To make it worse, Cordelia leads a group of girls in whatever affect she favors, putting Elaine doubly on edge.

Just as in this novel, I had a friend in junior high who terrified us with threats of exclusion. She was the arbiter of who would be invited to a sleepover or a Y dance. We had to do her bidding. We operated out of fear. By tenth grade she moved away and we were relieved. After all, none of us had the skills to disengage or call her out.

The women in this chapter have eventually awakened to the damage a wayward friend might bring to the friendship. Maximillian Holland in his book, *Social Bonding and Nurture Kinship*, points out the sociocultural aspects of bonding and how those relationships are not only biological, but also based on friendship. Women say their female friends are there for nurturing and support. In this chapter we've seen how one sided it can be and how the relationships can deteriorate or rupture. The person pushed out or who chooses to move away still feels scathed. Yet the choice to estrange is real and can be a step forward.

Let's consider the following questions as they apply to you.

Did you always suspect your friend was hiding something?

The evidence that your friend is troubled was most likely there for some time. Confronting her isn't easy but might be necessary.

Why are you in a friendship with someone who exhibits these behaviors?

Often we have a history with this friend or the level of friendship keeps us there. In specific instances, it would serve both of you to leave.

Is your friend at risk due to her patterns?

If so, being the responsible one can help her. This entails speaking to her family or spouse/partner in order to keep her safe.

Have you asked yourself why you want to be in this friendship and are you able to leave?

You have come to realize this is not a healthy set-up and need to have the courage to act on an exit strategy.

Do you feel you are saving yourself by distancing from the circumstance?

There is nothing that will change unless you take this step. Your friend cannot hear you nor can she help herself presently or change her pattern.

Are you relieved and do you have more clarity as you move toward a break?

In making this decision, you are preserving your self-esteem and your own personal values.

SHE SAID / SHE SAID

EXHIBIT B: Thin Ice: Instability

Celine and Brittany

In this exhibit, I have interviewed two women who have been best friends for over two decades. We'll focus first on Celine, 36, who recounts how her life and Brittany's crumbled at the age of eighteen. Brittany fell into serious drug use. Celine was pregnant and had a baby instead of starting college. Throughout years of rejection and mixed messages from their families, the two friends have carried each other.

Celine

> We were each other's only lifeline, only family.
> Then Brittany started using again. I kicked her out.
>
> •
>
> Brittany and I met in eighth grade and became best friends from the start. There were nasty girls and Brittany got into fistfights and when I wasn't there, it was a problem. We were a buffer for each other.
>   Together we cut classes and were not good students, it didn't matter to us. We smoked weed a little, smoked cigarettes and followed the boys. Lots of boy stuff. We went shopping and went to parties. We were so close, but not family friends. Our mothers knew each other but weren't friends although we were from the same

> background and religion. My mother was the cool mom. She tried to be friends with my friends but not in a good way. She tried to steal my friends. I took care of my siblings—Brittany was the only social life I had.

As Celine describes it, her mother was there but absent, living in her own world, meeting men online.

> Brittany is an only child. We always felt like sisters. It was a tight community where we grew up, in upstate New York. Everyone knew everyone.

Unsafe Ground

At present Celine is in the auto business and has two children. In 2008 she married her younger child's father and left her hometown for North Carolina. Although she and Brittany do not see each other often, they text daily and speak on the phone. When Celine reflects on Brittany's drug problem, she says she never saw it coming. In retrospect, as teenagers she and Brittany were at parties and it was difficult for Brittany to be sober in that environment.

> When I was pregnant with my son, Brittany was the only person there for me. It's also when I saw Brittany was high. That's when it hit me. But she'd been like this for years. Once I faced it, I began doing everything to help. While I have been supportive of Brittany, I never know if I'll get a call that she's in jail. Or dead. It's frustrating and scary. It puts a wedge between us.

Celine also knows Brittany's potential and believes in her friend. Their arguments are only about keeping Brittany on track and how to strive for a life beyond her addiction:

> Brittany and I needed each other. I mean I was close to my mother but looking back I see how toxic she was and how she tried to control every aspect of my life. I don't let her do that anymore. Today I'm close with my family while Brittany is not close at all with hers. That makes me think she needs me more.

Sheltering

At times Celine has invited Brittany to stay with her, to move in with her family when she had nowhere else to go. Yet the addiction remained and despite Brittany's assurances, she was still using drugs. This was too threatening to Celine:

> Things get bad between us when Brittany does something wrong and we have a big problem. First she rented a car while she was staying with me. The toll payments kept coming out of my bank account for months. It added up. That was the first part of it, then I found a needle cap in the bathroom because Brittany was using. I said to Brittany, I don't want drugs in my house and kicked her out. But I was so worried about where she'd end up and at the same time I had to look out for my family, my kids. I was torn and very sad. We had a breakup that lasted for a year.

The pressure placed on the healthy friend when her best friend engages in perilous behavior is tremendous. The wayward friend's problems bleed into all aspects of both friend's lives. This scenario played out for Brittany and Celine after the friends reconciled and there was an inciting incident. Brittany, while working on her sobriety, posted on Facebook that she had a new best friend. Not only was Celine irate, but this new friend of Brittany's was using and the concern was she would draw her downward, back to where she'd been:

> I felt like she'd taken advantage of me when she made that post. All our arguments are about drugs. When I saw Brittany's post, I told her it was insulting and that I am the one who has had her back all these years. That I didn't even know who this girl was.

Again, the friends didn't speak for over a year—the second go round of silence. Although Brittany said she understood Celine's position and apologized, claiming it was her fault, Celine felt mistrustful again:

> Brittany insisted she was sober at this point in time. It was just an error in judgment. But how will I ever know? Besides, because we are so close, I don't have any other female friends, and I don't want any others. People have let me down. A sober Brittany would never do that.

The Cloud

As Celine reports her ups and downs with Brittany, we see this is not based on the quality of the friendship, which is quite high. It is a 'circumstantial' cloud that hangs over the two women:

Whenever Brittany would slip back it was bad. She came from a good family, they had money, unlike mine. They sent her to rehab, they tried. She was in rehab when I got married. I tried to be supportive but I wished she could have been there. It wasn't easy.

When Brittany listens to me, when she means it, I feel like she'll be okay. I asked her to do an online college curriculum with me and she did it because I pushed. It's this sort of thing that gives me hope. I know what Brittany is capable of. Someone once told me that I give her all my energy and I get nothing back. It isn't like that at all. I just want her sober, for everything to lift and be safer.

Brittany

I definitely was not thinking when I posted about that other friend, who was a user. I look back and see it's hurtful. I keep forgetting people are waiting for me to fail again. The worst part is how it made Celine feel. I am empty without her, without the chance to talk with her.

•

The first fight Celine and I ever had was over a boy when we were fifteen. We both liked the same boy. We both got him because one of us hooked up with him first and then he moved on to the best friend. He did it, he pitted us against each other, he thought we'd fall apart over him. It went on for a few days and then we saw it was his fault, not ours. We stopped it right then and put each other first, it was a lesson about our friendship.

Rabbit Hole

Brittany, 36, a former security guard is married with three children. Presently, due to a setback, she is living in a shelter and her children are living with her mother in Sharon, Connecticut. From the start of my interview with both women, I was struck by how through years of dejection, tough times and mixed support from their families, she and Celine have remained friends. All the same, Brittany's addiction and hope of a steadfast recovery remain challenging and at the center of the friendship.

> Celine was there when I started hanging out with people who used. First it was weed and then cocaine and then heroin. Celine was the only person who was supporting me, begging for me to stop, once it began. There was a group of friends who were making it worse. But I had grown up with a real childhood. I came from a nice family. My father had a good job, I was spoiled but I was on my own. When we were kids we'd go to 7-11 or to Celine's house because my mother would ask 101 questions for my friend to enter. I couldn't bring anyone home to hang out.
>
> Today I'm in recovery. I've been sober for over a year and am working to get my children back. My mother has custody and I know she takes care of them but I never really got along with her. I wanted her to love me, but it didn't feel like she did. It worries me when it comes to my kids. It is Celine who is the one I count on. I've had to go through family court. At the moment it's hard, I am with my husband but not with my kids. Celine gets to see them, she travels to visit. I tell myself if I can stay clean, I can have a life with them and my husband.

Belief

Brittany feels alienated from her mother, whom she tells us is jealous of her friendship with Celine. Both Celine and Brittany share feelings that fall into the fictive family mode that I wrote about earlier. Celine represents a big sister. Brittany describes her as seeming older and more responsible although they are the same age. They offer each other a sense of protection despite what they are up against.

> My mother has told me to stay away from Celine. When I was pregnant with my youngest, my mom called her and said to leave me alone. She doesn't see how Celine helps. Meanwhile, Celine is the only person in my life who has helped me totally. We used to laugh about how strict our families were, old fashioned really. Plus my mother always wanted to impress everyone, maybe that's why I'm like this, so no one is impressed.
>
> I would have done anything with Celine leading; she is that kind of person. She knew I had a history of drug use and she kept leading me toward a better life, toward the light. It hasn't been easy. The heroin has gotten between us. Also, I fall for the wrong people. That's why the whole incident with Celine trying to keep me from the wrong people was so upsetting. I posted about this woman who tried to get me to use again. She was lying to me. It made me realize how I've been in the past, asking for money. Now I know what it's like when I used people for my habit. Except I'm aware and I cut ties with her. I've promised Celine I can't be distracted.
>
> Celine is the only person there for me through everything. That's why when we get into arguments it

hurts the most. We stopped talking because I'd hurt her feelings and she thought there could be a relapse. When we stopped talking it made it worse. But I stayed sober.

Reunion

Being apart from Celine has been difficult for Brittany. She describes their separations as 'heartbreak,' and periods of peace, when Brittany is sober and they can respect one another, as 'feeling safe.'

> We look like each other, sound like each other. We are best friends in every way. Even though I put her through hell and have not been a friend she can count on. It was the longest time we'd ever stayed apart and argued. We missed each other. It went on for months and felt like a real break up. It was so lonely for me. We had to count more on our husbands. Both are nice husbands, they understand our friendship, but it wasn't like talking to your best friend.
>
> What never changes is how we talk about our children, our hopes for them. Celine and I will always have the same taste in music, rap, eighties music, even the food we like is the same. We used to trade recipes, everything we cook is Italian. We share what we watch streaming. We dress alike, always in leggings and t-shirts. My thing with shirts has rubbed off on Celine.

Goals

An important aspect of recovery for women being treated for substance use disorders is social support, according to an abstract, "The Relationship Changed Because I Had Changed" by Kelner and Gavriel-Fried. This certainly applies to the Brittany/Celine couplet, where the foundation of their friendship is a safety net.

It is worth noting the goals of both friends. For Brittany, we know she depends on Celine as her life coach:

> I vent with her about being judged, I laugh with her. When I tell her something, I know she can be trusted. We can be honest about our husbands with one another and both of us are happily married now. I am godmother to Celine's daughter. I just hope to God we do not get into another fight. I can be hot headed, out of anger. And I need to not do that and to take responsibility for what I did in the past.

Celine reports that she feels completely understood by Brittany:

> Brittany is there for me, in my life. She really gets it, plus we've been bfs all these years. My kids call her Aunt Brittany. I hope in outpatient she knows there is consequential thinking. That the clinic has changed her mentality. I want to be a model for her since I rarely drink and don't do drugs. That it's the right way.

Can This Friendship Be Saved?

According to a Pew Research Center study, forty-six percent of Americans have a close friend or family member who is addicted to drugs or was at one point in their life. We know how taxing it is to stay with this person and the value in leaving for the nonuser, being Celine in this case. At the same time, because Celine is a constant in Brittany's life, during her recovery, she kept her from a new friend, a user who threatened Brittany's success and healthy future.

After a major breakup over Brittany's addiction, today she and Celine are reconciled. Brittany has been sober for the past thirteen months and talks to Celine daily about plans for the future. This includes how she'll care for her family after four years of being apart and how unnerving it is if she and Celine are not on good terms. Celine describes their connection as "so close that we lift each other up," but also acknowledges how disruptive their fights can be. Her fear is that Brittany will not live up to her potential. Celine's requirement for the friendship to prevail is that Brittany is not using drugs.

CHAPTER THREE

A Diametrically Opposed Friend

Do you assume you and this friend will always be in same phase of life?

Is this friend supposed to always agree with you?

Have you become competitive about your changing view?

Are you part of a larger group of women friends?

Has the trust eroded between the two of you?

If any of the questions above resonate for you, then you and your friend may have had unrealistically high expectations for the friendship:

> Since you and your best friend have arrived in a new town, you have found solace in one another. Your values are similar and you have always been totally open with her. It has been a happy coincidence that as the years have gone on, your children who are similar ages, get

along. There are co-family events and everyone seems delighted. Lately you have confided in her. First that you are not happy at work and she has been sympathetic. You reveal that your mother-in-law expects you to stay put because your present position is flexible in terms of the kids after school schedule. Your best friend dismisses that, having moved to a new company about a year ago. She is a guide on how to finesse this. She's so on target and there for you, it's almost as if you're sisters. She's your family and you are hers. Perhaps you whine too much, but she's patient and totally supportive when you actually do move on and begin another position.

But now you are unhappy in your marriage and she does not want to hear about it. The idea of it offends her. In her own life, she is all in: her husband, children. She chooses to be with friends in cohesive marriages only and she can't lend an ear or be nonjudgmental. Haven't you always been there for each other, under any circumstance? In retrospect, you were more open-minded, you knew the two of you were never twins, just on a similar path at the same time. When she tells you to stay with your husband for the sake of the family, she isn't l listening to how you feel. Why doesn't she understand this as your bf—why is she annoyed that you are in an unhappy marriage?

Teetering

Women's desire for close female friends isn't only cultural, it's chemical. In *The Gendered Society*, Michael Kimmel writes that when women are involved with one another, they "… release oxytocin, which produces a calming effect and a desire for closeness." On screen we've been shown what rewarding friendships provide and the buoyancy women offer one another. These come in a variety of flavors including *Sweet Magnolias* where three high school best friends carry each other through the challenges of adulthood, love, career and children, to *Someone Great*, a romantic comedy that emphasizes how women friends support one another through the darkest days, to *Good Girls*. In this series three suburbanite mothers in the Midwest rob a supermarket and then end up working for a mob gang. As their world gets more tangled, their connection grows stronger—all for the greater good—that of family and financial stability.

According to my interviewees, many of us have a trusted, dependable friend. They are on the same timetable as we are, the closeness and identity proves reassuring. Often they're at the same stage of life in terms of career, marriage, house purchasing, children, divorce, singlehood—any of our life-changing experiences—it makes the friendship deeply compatible. There isn't any drama, only support and a shared worldview. Unless one of the two friends changes her path and becomes a **diametrically opposed friend**. Then the balance is off and a rift is almost inevitable.

Kimberly, 29, lives in Denver and owns an online business selling makeup products. She and her best friend were business partners for several years.

> We split up after an argument, a decision about the business that we viewed differently. We couldn't find a common ground and it tore us apart. I told her it wouldn't be okay with her approach and she didn't like mine.
>
> This break up lasted a half-year and now we are speaking but it is nothing like before. When we weren't talking, I used to cry, so at least we've patched it up. We

used to share secrets and now we just ask how the other is doing. I had no one else to talk to or be with the way we had been together. Of all my friends, she was the closest to me. Our backgrounds, schooling, our parents, are the same.

Now we both have our own businesses and the friendship is changed, the closeness is lost. When we first fell out, our mothers were both so upset and suggested we give it time. My mother said to me that things will fall into place. Things happen, there should be time to heal. I know one thing; I would not go into business again with her, ever.

To avoid drama and disappointment, Scarlet, 36, a paralegal in Washington State, has determined to keep a complicated friendship going at all costs:

What happened a few years ago with a top-of-the-list friend almost destroyed me. She began dating someone who didn't like me and poisoned her against me. We had been such close friends for so many years, I couldn't let it go. When she left that man, I was there, I hung on. I know where I stand. It has to do with who influences her. I know she counts more for me than I do for her. I tell myself if we aren't separated, it's fine.

Josey, 23, an accountant from South Carolina, laments losing a friendship with a shared history at the center:

She knows all my secrets and I worry about that since she could hurt me. We used to understand things and agree until we had a falling out. We are from the same background and that helped us get through being so far from home these past ten years. That's why when I met a man and started dating him, my friend was so unhappy with me. He is not from our background and that matters to her. Since we aren't together my life isn't as clear and focused. It's not easy for me.

Friend Blame

These moving parts in an intimate friendship are unnerving. After all, these friends have been steady and strong. Jeffrey Werden, a psychoanalyst who practices in New York City and Westchester County, tells us close friends fill a void. "There is a soothing, reassuring part to being in the inside circle. Women form pairs and groups as a way to affirm themselves. Female friends of any age like it when they are similar in terms of ambition, values and experiences." Elizabeth J. Aries and Fern L. Johnson in their abstract "The Talk of Women Friends" note the differences between how men and women approach these relationships. They found that women talk about personal issues with their female friends more frequently than do men with their male friends, trading confidences when it comes to their intimate feelings. Because women are facile at self-disclosure, they are willing to spill their inner-most longings and hopes. In this exchange, they are rewarded with a compassionate response.

As the friendship begins to fray, women report tensions with the one person they feel was a sure bet, a steady and loyal friend. The emotional turmoil is sensed on both sides. What makes it so painful is how the friendships unravel despite that shared feelings are in place.

Larissa, 39, a single physician's assistant living in the southwest, found that her married friends' life choices also affected their relationship with her:

> I want to be with friends who have the lifestyle I have. Ten years ago, it didn't matter who was with someone and who wasn't, how we lived. Now I don't want to be with friends who are running around with their young children, figuring out a school calendar with their husbands. They look at me as if something is wrong with me, as a person and as their friend. They've no idea what my life is about, what means something to me. Only my friends whose lifestyles are like mine get it.

Agnes, 50, a teacher from Wisconsin, saw her best friend drift away from her when she got divorced:

> For years we were best friends. Then I wasn't married anymore. We'd make plans, she'd cancel. She'd wait for a better plan, may the best plan win. We joined a reading group together but she was mean-spirited. She told me my partner was a loser. What could I do? Only she had the great husband, a perfect man. After I reached out and she ignored me, I knew I didn't want to be friends with her. I am relieved finally. I know she judged me all the time once we weren't "twins."

While I was conducting my research and interviewing women during Covid, I heard of breaches in important friendships when it came to vaccinations. This applied not only to the personal decision of the friends, but for their children as well. As we know, the vaccinations and boosters represented more than simply a health measure. They were loaded issues. Some friendships couldn't withstand the choice their friends made versus their own opinions when it came to this. Consider the women's narratives below:

Although Jolie, 33, working in a medical lab and living in Vermont, laments that she no longer speaks to her best childhood friend, she also feels it was inevitable:

> When I was 25, I had a best friend. We'd grown up together. She was single and I was single. Now she has a four-year old daughter and I have two small kids. Something happened and she said I should let it go. I usually do, but it had to do with how I live and what I eat, how I look at life. She doesn't believe in any kind of vaccination or Covid boosters. She refused to get her children vaccinated for even the flu. I work in the medical field, and I know what these viruses can do. I explained this but she didn't care. After an up and down period we never spoke again over what she said and her worldview. We had been very good friends for years. Our kids played together. But these shots came between us. I say to myself, we all have someone we broke up with, don't we? It was awful when it happened and it's awful now.

For Monica, 30, a teacher's aide and single mother living in Montana, vaxxing/boosting was the final straw:

> My BFF from kindergarten and high school and I did not see eye to eye. She was a naturalist and did not vaccinate her kids. I told her during Covid our kids couldn't hang out together. She said the shots, including boosters, caused autism and I didn't believe it. It was a big deal between us. I was afraid to be with someone non-vaccinated. Working in the schools, I knew all the

children and teachers and administrators had to be vaccinated. She sent her kids to school and told them it was a religious reason why her children were not vaccinated which was a lie.

    Even before Covid, she was critical of what I did, what formula I used, that I used disposable diapers and sent my kids to daycare. She stopped talking to me out of nowhere after we had a discussion over immunizations. I got tired of defending. She said I needed to read more about immunizations for children and I said I trusted doctors. We grew apart. It was over as far as I'm concerned. I'd say hello if I saw her, but nothing is what it was.

Lucy, 32, a dental hygienist in Santa Fe, also had a fall out over vaccinations and boosting with an important friend, along with voting decisions:

There was all this friction over the presidential election, we voted for opposite parties. Neither of us liked how that felt. It didn't seem real that these serious topics and choices could come between us. But they did. We'd gone to college together, we'd lived in the same dorm. We had been close for years. What was strange was how my friend didn't mind that we fought over this, she could shrug it off. But I couldn't. We disagreed about vaxxing too. That was the worst thing that happened. She was an anti-vaxxer—for anything. We really had words over immunizing our little kids. It became a nightmare. I thought we'd never work it out, never be close again.

    Today we speak but it has a stilted feel to it. Like we are too different after once being the same. The link is missing.

Nina, 46, working in the tech industry with a teenage son, living in the Southeast, is comfortable with the outcome of her friendship over her anti-vaxxing stance:

> My friend and I had quite a history together. We knew each other from our single days and rarely disagreed. Since we're in the same industry, we were lucky to avoid competition. Instead we really understood and cared what opportunities came along for each other. Every Sunday we'd go running together and talk about everything. When people began being vaccinated, it was my choice to not do it. I didn't want my son or my husband to do it either. She was so offended. She insinuated I was ignorant and stubborn. My husband and son ended up getting their boosters and it didn't break up our family. But this friend and I, who were always on the same page, were ruined. She called me to say how wrong I was, how foolish my decision was. Maybe she was ready to drop me, except after that conversation, I wanted nothing to do with her. She couldn't respect my decision.

Friends with Money

When friends differ in terms of their financial situations, it can drive a wedge in the relationship. This falls into the category of diametrically opposed friends because money can change the very essence of a friendship. For the friend without very comfortable finances, there is the scurrying around to become like her friends with money. For the friend with money, there can be an ambition to be only with friends in a similar social strata. Kristin Wong writes in her *New York Times* piece, "Your Friend

Has More Money Than You Do. How Can Your Relationship Survive?": "Financial disparities in friendships can create an unease where one shouldn't exist, especially when people conflate their net worth with their self-worth."

Consider the 2006 film with the same name as this section, *Friends with Money*. Olivia, played by Jennifer Aniston, is a housecleaner who was once a teacher. Her friends, played by Joan Cusack, Catherine Keener and Frances McDormand, are wealthy women who seem to have no troubles. Except of course they do, including how they parent their children, identity troubles, and marital troubles. We see in this movie how money as a consuming desire can cause tension. Aniston's character, Olivia, is obsessed with what she is denied and while she cares about her friends, there is always her urge to keep up and her resentment that she cannot. Her wealthy friends view her with pity and take her in, but only to some extent. In this manner, the incompatibility is obvious and uneasy.

In real life, consider Bailey, 37, who values her wealthy friends. A fundraiser, living in New Mexico, she is partnered and has twin sons. She has social aspirations that she herself describes as 'maniacal':

> I was hoping to know the right people always. I had to wait until our family had enough money that it would be reciprocated. Except there is always someone who has more money, a more beautiful home and better things. My best friend, Jillie, told me my values were twisted but I didn't listen. We had met through this clique of friends when we were teenagers. We did all the daring things but in a spoiled way. After that she sort of snapped out of it and became serious. She went to law school and now she works for a not for profit. But I clung to the women

friends who have the best lifestyle. I became more involved with a moneyed world. I was engaged to a man from a very wealthy family and how they lived changed my view. It made me more interested in being a one percenter. We called off the wedding and that's fine. I've kept the 'money as power' part of it. I have dropped two men who were serious about me because of money and two women friends who seemed to only care about the money part.

Today I'm with a man who has money and still I wonder sometimes if it's enough, if I should have chosen someone richer. My girlfriends are wealthy and so are the men they're with. A few of my new friends I've met through my children. Today Jillie doesn't speak to me. I'm hurt but mostly I'm planning this rarified life.

Friend Divorce

In this chapter we see that whatever the issue is, once friends are no longer on the same path, the friendship can't be sustained. Add to the equation that these pairs of friends often describe themselves as family. Then it's a double whammy, they are losing a best friend who feels like a sister. In the above interviews, the friendship proves fragile after certain incidents.

In an article in the *Atlantic*, "How Friendships Change in Adulthood," William Rawlins, a professor at Ohio University, remarks that, "Friendships are always susceptible to circumstances." Aminatou Sow and Ann Friedman in their book, *Big Friendship: How We Keep Each Other Close*, detail the frustrations of female friendships. They describe it as "The dynamic of pushing each other away even as we're trying to reconnect.

The struggle is to find true peace with a long-term friendship that is changing."

Several interviewees have lamented they ever expressed their true thoughts to a friend because it triggered the beginning of the end. The destructive episode affects both women. For the person pushed away, the **estrangee**, the suffering is acute. For the **estranger**, who is deliberately separating from the friend, it might be a relief, but it can also be filled with distress and emotion.

For Layla, 50, living in Washington State, where she works in the food industry, the 'friend divorce' was about loyalty:

> I understand why my best friend has left me and we are 'divorced.' We come from a small town, we grew up together, like our mothers and grandmothers. All these generations of friends. So when this friend and her husband were separated, I got her through the weekends that her kids were with their father and she had no plans. We sat and watched Golden Girls and talked about what a cad she was married to. Then they got back together and she never forgave me for what I said.

Like Layla, Steffi, 41, from a Midwestern city, working as a graphic designer, is also no longer in touch with her best friend:

> She and I go way back. She was pregnant at sixteen and then had the second kid at the same time I had my first child. I even took care of her when she was pregnant with her first child. My parents took her in because her mother was always working. She'd come home from school to my house. As teenage girls we went to the park, the mall, the movies together. We had the same group of

friends. She was always thinner. I'm educated, I pursued my education. She chose to have children earlier instead. She also thinks moms should stay at home with their kids. We never agreed on that. It was like out of nowhere our points of view changed. We stopped talking because we couldn't agree. Thankfully I'd moved to another city when the breakup happened. We were no longer a block away and it's only through my mother that I've heard about her lately. This was an emotional loss. We were such good friends. It is so hard for me to handle.

Women who end up as 'diametrically opposed friends' report it happens over politics, world view, life choices and ambition. Once their values collide and are no longer the same, the friendship is put to the test. This phenomenon, more prevalent than ever in our divided times, has triggered questions about how well the friends knew and understood each other from the start.

The Ramifications

The idea of conflicting political beliefs as a deal breaker among friends and a requisite to establishing new friends has been at a high since the 2016 election. In 2020, NPR's *All Things Considered* did a segment on how politics harm family and friendships. They reported that political rifts have become about differences "of basic morality, core values and character," referencing the Pew Research Center's finding that almost 80% of Americans presently have "just a few" or no friends across the aisle in terms of political leanings.

In contrast is a piece that ran in *Psychology Today* by Todd B. Kashdan, "Why Are You Rethinking Friendships Because of

Politics?" The article defines the features of solid friendship as: a goal of pleasure, meaning both parties appreciate each other's company, a sense of duty, where the expectation is for friends to act in each other's best interests and that a level of empathy exists, requiring both sides to "understand each other's perspective" and motivations. Kashdan emphasizes in these cases that friends find a way to agree, "when discord arises," rather than relationships being "contingent" on who someone votes for.

These opposing views can apply to differing life choices as well as to political leanings.

For example, Liv, 31, from Vail, Colorado and her treasured friend were deeply affected by no longer being on concurrent paths. Presently Liv is located in the northeast and engaged. She and this friend were locked in a back and forth until it was finally resolved.

> I had a friend, June, I met her in college twelve years ago. We were connected by our faith. We had similar upbringings. We were late bloomers and we learned together about guys. We would talk and talk about it. After school I moved to Philadelphia, and she moved to her hometown.
>
> Over the last years, things shifted and I no longer believed that I had to wait until I was married to have sex. June wanted to wait until she was married and was concerned and frustrated with me. I was hurt that she didn't approve. Aren't you worth more than that, don't you want a better path, a different experience, she asked. This is going to cause you heartbreak she said when we talked about it long distance.
>
> Our conversations became less frequent. I would have

new revelations in how I chose to live while she found it threatening. June married someone I did not feel great about. I was at her wedding. I should not have expressed what I thought of her husband. When I met my fiance and was falling in love with him, it was a departure. He is agnostic although he grew up in a traditional religious home. I wish he could be attached to his religion, but he had a super different upbringing. He and I moved in together and June asked what was I doing, weren't he and I just dating. That felt like another stern fracture. Her message was that she and I are not the same anymore and couldn't be friends. Her faith had deepened while mine had not. She will not be attending my wedding because I will not be inviting her. It was that kind of break up, I cannot be in this friendship."

In an article in *Psychology Today*, "The Importance of Female Friendships Among Women," Kristen Fuller notes that women "thrive on strong relationships with their girlfriends" and are an emotional support system for one another. For those who are no longer in our lives, there is a sense of recurring loss. We experience this and see it in real time with the narratives in *Estranged*, but also in fiction. *Sula* by Toni Morrison comes to mind. Both Sula and Nel come from a community called The Bottom. As young girls, Sula is independent and bold, Nel is reticent and polite. Their friendship runs deep until they are adult women on distinct paths and all that they share is put to the test. In *Who Will Run the Frog Hospital* by Lorrie Moore we meet Berie and her best friend Sils. As high school girls in upstate New York working at a summer job, they are insulated. Until Sill gets into trouble and Berie must help her. Afterward the connection is in turmoil and as the years go on, they cannot recreate the bond.

Another narrative where the two friends became too disparate is recounted by Violet. Violet is 33 and lives in Boston where she works in marketing:

> Recently I had an abortion although I deeply want to be a mother. It was sad for me even if I expected it to be sad. My boyfriend was supportive and wonderful but the experience was brutal. At this time, his whole career kicked in and he was very busy, and that made it more difficult. My friend was very kind during this period—we had been together for decades.
>
> There was another big issue that harmed our friendship that happened before the abortion. There was a party hosted by mutual friends for this friend. I flew to be there for her. Her husband was not friendly to me, he was mean. It was another crazy, biting event where I felt I didn't belong. I felt like I was an embarrassment and I didn't fit in anymore. By then our relationship was in such pain.
>
> I thought maybe we could be close, but not with how different our paths were. I had no idea how it could be working for us. She said to me, "You don't want to be friends anymore." We spoke about how things have really shifted for me. I realized I'm worthy of so much more. It was exhausting since we stopped speaking the same language. And know we cannot invest in this friendship going forward. That was what we decided.

Sister Splits

For the sister interview in this chapter, I'd like to point out that Alex, 67, retired from work as a graphic designer, comes from a divided family of five sisters. She lives in North Carolina:

> What started as a tiff at a card game at my cousin's turned into a family feud. This was eight years ago. My older sister, Stella, walked out and we have not spoken since. We are the opposite in terms of religious and political beliefs. Our mother was upset that my sister and I fought so much and she was grateful whenever we did things together. But Stella was always the ugly duckling and depressed without knowing it. She couldn't believe someone asked her to marry him. He was a lifeline for her, she was rescued. My other sisters and I watched while she later wised up to who he was, but she stayed. Where could she go? None of us liked him. I saw he was awful from the start. Growing up she was on the other side of me and our three sisters.
>
> She and I never got along and we'd have these fist fights when we were kids. My other sisters and I were skinny and svelte, she wasn't. Our mother was mad at herself for marrying our father, we weren't raised in a tight family. There was no praise or love or guidance. I left home when I was twenty.
>
> I didn't consider my sister once I was gone. My younger sisters and I have so much in common. After I moved out, Stella tossed all my stuff out that I'd left there. She figured I wasn't ever coming home. She had no right to grab and toss it. She has a real mean streak.
>
> It took years but finally our mother stopped caring if we were close. This was odd only because she was

so close to all her sisters. Stella was always envious of me and is to this day. That's the problem, we can't get beyond it so we can't be together.

After the argument that night, my other sisters tried to make it better with Stella. They asked her to talk with me, but she wouldn't. I wasn't interested either. We'd done nothing but hurt each other and be nasty from the time we were kids. Even as adults with our mother in this social setting we couldn't be civilized. We have no thoughts about the world that are the same, ever. My other sisters spend time with her and care about her. They spend time with me too. But Stella and I do not speak and I doubt we will.

Dissolutions

When an entire friend group or family is involved, the reactions of the other women can also have an influence on the quarrelling parties. With three other sisters who refused to side with Alex or Stella, they were alone in their feud. The noise belonged to the two of them and the rift festered. As Marion McCue de Velez, a social worker, tells us, "Women often tiptoe around what they want to say to each other, knowing their friend or sister will listen only if it doesn't seem too critical. Encouragement is fine, but finding fault is not. Loading on too much is a risk to the relationship."

If we think of series that show both positive and negative aspects of our female friends, *Big Little Lies* (2017 to 2019) comes to mind. The cast includes Reese Witherspoon, Nicole Kidman, Laura Dern, Zoe Kravitz and Shalane Woodard. Tensions run high in this tony town. There are secrets among a group of mothers who claim to be friends. But what is loyalty among them when it comes to murder? In *Desperate Housewives* (2004 to 2012), the rivalries and divisions among the women in suburbia bounce about per episode. Always it seems there is an odd woman out. In both dramas the friends have complicated if privileged lives. They are in search of a safe haven without knowing how to protect themselves and who to trust.

The American Perspectives Study found that while women are more satisfied with how many friends they have and the level of emotional support received than are men, fewer Americans have a best friend today. However, the more friends we have, the more satisfied we are. Thus, when there are histrionics, followed by distancing and loss, the results can be profound.

How do these questions apply to you?

Is this the only close friend where you have been alike in your approach to situations and do you share a belief system?

This might be the right time to weigh what the friendship means to you and what you expect as your paths diverge. Does the friendship mean more than your differences?

Are you able to reacclimate in hopes the friendship isn't lost?

Some of us are more acrobatic than others. At this juncture, you can decide what makes you want to preserve the friendship despite the direction your friend has chosen.

Do you feel that forgiveness or an apology is in order?

If the friendship has lost its center, some women feel they need to be acknowledged in order to have one last try.

Why is it a requirement that you and your friend share a path?

It is worth asking yourself why it matters that your friend no longer subscribes to the same beliefs you once shared. Is this enough to cause a break in the friendship?

Is there no foundation in the friendship beyond what you have in common?

There are plenty of friendships where the friends are unalike on many levels and the friendship prospers. You might want to reconsider the friend's new life and discuss how you feel before you announce it is finite.

Are you sure you are not selling the friendship out?

If you cannot abide your friend's behavior and choice, the friendship is essentially over.

SHE SAID / SHE SAID

EXHIBIT C: Ambitions Collide

Helen and Gabriella

Having listened to both Helen and Gabriella's account of what happened between them, I realized how heartfelt it is when one friend changes course. Helen, 57, who narrates below, expected her friendship with Gabriella to last a lifetime. Instead they ended up "diametrically opposed friends."

Helen

> I asked her why she had done it and she called me 'garbage.' A bf calling you that? Afterward we avoided each other. We never spoke again.

•

> When I first got to Atlanta thirty years ago, I wanted my friends to be from back home, from Antigua. That's how I met Gabriella, that's how we helped each other at the beginning. We were both single, looking for dependable jobs. What was offered to women from the Caribbean was work as nannies, cooks or housekeepers. Everything was unknown and we were far from home. We were in a tight knit circle. I was like a big sister to Gabriella. I helped her find her first job.

Helen's search for friendship as a source of social support and belonging, and a substitute for family, is a common thread in this study. Interviewees often remark that because their friends are a choice, not assigned like family, they expect more from them. From the start, Helen and Gabriella provided solace for each other. Helen knew the value of women in her life and Gabriella was someone she had sought out.

> It was the nineties, you were supposed to get married, have kids, have a house. Gabriella wanted the whole deal and when it didn't work out, she was angry that I was okay without it, I didn't count on a man. I didn't care while she did. By the end, we had different hopes and plans. We fought over it. Afterward we avoided each other. All because we stopped agreeing.

Breakage

Presently Helen works for a family and lives in Georgia. While she is proud of raising her children as a single mother she is sad that she and Gabriella have not spoken in over ten years. Nonetheless she is comfortable with her opinion she expressed decades ago about Gabriella's love life. What happened with Gabriella has impacted Helen's decisions in her friendships going forward:

> In the beginning there would be parties on the weekends and barbeques. Gabriella and I did it all together. People thought we were sisters, we acted like we were. That's why I was the one who told Gabriella what I thought. With her first boyfriend she was his revenge relationship and I saw he wasn't in love with her. It wasn't right. I told her the truth, he lied about things. As close as we had become, we didn't agree. At that point we stuck together anyway, like family.

Although Helen was vocal about Gabriella's choice of a partner and did not support her decision, when it came to her plans for a career, from the start Helen was respectful. She knew what it meant to Gabriella to earn her degree and become a teacher. What weighed down their friendship were the men in Gabriella's life.

After Helen advised Gabriella to let the first man go, there were red flags with the next man:

> Gabriella didn't want to hear it but with the second guy, I really saw things. When they got engaged I thought he wasn't the right person for her. He had an agenda and

then they had a baby. She was in a rage, she wanted to marry him and I worried about it. I spoke up about that.

The friendship soldiered on, despite a brewing tension:

Gabriella made a bridesmaid list and I was not on it, maybe because of what I saw in her fiancé. Or she thought I wasn't looking good—she was thinner. I didn't forget but I never told her how slighted I felt. What I told her was how this man moved from one girl to another. She had issues with him but was going forward. There was an engagement party, a shower. We were still in our 'Antigua family.' Soon after the wedding was off and it was rough for her.

At this juncture for Helen, there was clearly a sense that her situation with Gabriella had changed. It was as if she no longer counted:

I look back and it had been building up—it had been too much. We were working at the same job—she was part time and I was full time. She'd be in the kitchen on the phone with her friend and wouldn't talk to me. She wouldn't even say hi, she had become rude and unfriendly. I had listened to her about the men, for years we had talked about it. But she was never there for me the same way. A lot went on for a long time—I covered for her with the men, with her schooling—we had been really, really close friends.

Finale

A year after the friction over Gabriella's fiancé, a drama of another kind occurred. Gabriella made a comment to Helen's sister, which felt like betrayal to Helen:

> I wasn't at my sister's one day and Gabriella was. She said negative things about me when I wasn't there to explain. My sister said that wasn't what a friend would do. A few days later I confronted Gabriella. We stood alone in the house where we both worked part time together. No one else was there. I said she'd gone too deep, saying this to my own sister, who no matter what would back me up. That's when she called me "garbage," that's when it was over.

For a year, Helen was plagued with questions about why Gabriella had sold her out, why the abrupt ending? With all that occurred, what hurt Helen the most was that without the friendship, she was not invited to Gabriella's daughter's first communion.

Helen never expected her friendship with Gabriella to be in jeopardy. She was astonished at how their fight escalated and how it damaged their relationship. Her schism with Gabriella has affected her view of other female friendships:

> I'm a certain age and I know what kind of friends I want. What happened with Gabriella has changed how I am with friends. I'm sure she has her own friends—we don't have any in common anymore. I stay more with cousins and my sisters and not as many friends as before. The older you get the more you put things in the past and

move on. I've learned I don't need a friend to get to know myself better. I know myself by myself, on my own.

Today I look back and see Gabriella and I were supposed to have done better. I always wonder when a relationship doesn't work out how we move on. I wouldn't go back, I don't think so. There was too much injury at the time. We helped each other, that has always mattered. There was something about Gabriella.

Gabriella

I thought we were good. I had no idea we were about to have a scene that would ruin our friendship.

•

I made new girlfriends when I got to the states because it was something I wanted. We were all similar, from Antigua and looking for work. Being in touch with Helen, who would hear about jobs, made things easier from the start. In Atlanta we were in the same group and invited to the same parties. She knew everyone and people looked to her for information, to meet and be included. She counted in our community. We became very close, people thought we were sisters.

Gain/Loss

Gabriella, 53, as a single mother and teacher, still questions how their friendship went wrong. Her intention was to move to the states for the right life. Friendships were made and lost along the way, but her connection to Helen was distinctive. She and Helen looked out for each other. Thirty years ago, they had the same point of view.

Although today the friends no longer speak, Gabriella and Helen had once shared a significant level of trust:

> Helen was a big part of my life when I met my first boyfriend. It was a serious relationship, we were together for a few years. I had started night classes, hoping to get my teaching degree and work at a school. Helen was one of the friends I saw during this period—when I had very little free time. When she and I talked about my goals, she liked that I was doing it. She also let me know my boyfriend wasn't right for me. I didn't want to admit having this man around changed things. Helen and I had been so close.

Careening

When Gabriella started seeing a second man, Helen became more outspoken than anyone else:

> I couldn't hear what Helen thought. Soon I was pregnant and my daughter was born. In the end, I didn't marry this man. It was a tough time for me. It was clear that Helen saw things another way. She wasn't one to get sidetracked by a man. Her view was that being a mother, having work and friendship should be enough. It started to feel different with her.

The week of the 'breakup' with Helen was meant to be an easy stretch for Gabriella. School was closed and she had time off from work for Christmas:

Helen's sister had invited people over for a holiday meal. Helen wasn't there when I made a remark about how she was always late for work. By nature I'm always on time and we were at the same job. It was such stupid stuff, I should have spoken with Helen directly about it—maybe she didn't want her sister to know. Maybe her sister criticized her because I'd said something.

A few days later she said to me, "Don't you realize we aren't friends anymore? If you have anything bad to say about me, say it to me and not through my sister." I was taken aback, shocked really. She said it again, "Don't you realize we aren't friends anymore?" It hurt me. It was too much like high school. I didn't answer her as I should have that day. Instead, I lost it, I lashed out, I went on and on. I said "I didn't know that because I got you this job a few months ago, I brought you in as a friend."

Friendship Precipice

Gabriella's experience with Helen reminds us of what goes on in a committed relationship—without the obligatory 'ending' conversation. What resonates is the intimacy, the reveal of ourselves, the rewards of time and energy lavished on the other person. While much has been written about what distinguishes these two types of bonds, in either case, we are drawn to the other person. The salient requirements of respect, honesty and loyalty apply to both.

Helen and Gabriella's friendship, filled with promise and a true rapport, was at a breaking point. The protective layering they had provided for each other was gone. Not only were their lives veering in different directions but after their confrontation, they were not physically planted in the same place.

> My school schedule changed right after our fight and I wasn't overlapping with Helen anymore at my part time job. I think that made it harder to fix, we weren't together for work anymore. I knew it should not have happened like this but there was nothing I could do. It was very upsetting, I felt as if we'd been torn apart.

The Aftermath

Gabriella wasn't afraid of running into Helen, but she did avoid walking by Helen's sister's home:

> I wondered what her sister had told her. To this day I would love to know. Maybe I should have asked Helen directly, maybe I should have gone back to her. I regret I didn't take those steps. We ended badly. We never even called each other. We left it at that.
>
> I didn't see Helen again except for two times. Once on the street with the little boy she watched. He was in a stroller and I said hi to him, but not to her. Then in a shop and I thought maybe she'd be receptive, but she wasn't. We did not say hello to each other. During that period, acquaintances we shared asked why I wasn't with her. I never said how we failed, but I kept thinking about that day when she asked, don't you realize we aren't friends anymore?

With her busy teaching schedule and daughter's schedule, time passed and Gabriella began with a new circle of friends. Antigua, the community where everyone was from, wasn't as important as it had been in the beginning. The world was opening up. Yet she regrets that her daughter and Helen's children were not part of their lives as they grew up.

Recently Gabriella received praise from the department for her work as a pre-K teacher and was sorry she couldn't share her success with Helen:

> Sometimes I wonder if it could be my fault. I've had some upsetting experiences with friends. What went on with Helen was a misunderstanding that got out of control. I'm very quiet but if someone gets me on the wrong side, I'll say more than I should.
>
> After this, I became more guarded about my women friends. I'm careful, not as open, because of Helen. I don't trust anyone else the same way I trusted Helen. For close to twenty years we had done things together, it was Helen I missed. Our friendship stopped abruptly, I didn't see it coming. I couldn't quite believe I'd never spend time with her again. I still don't know why she said what she said, why it ended as it did. I have no hard feelings toward her. It wasn't a friendship where the friends steal your husband or boyfriend. I know this is something that should have worked out. We learn as we grow older. We learn what mattered all along.

Can This Friendship Be Saved?

The outcome of the Helen/Gabriella story is one of loss on both sides. The two friends were already struggling with their friendship when Helen's sister became part of the mix, fueling the fire. And here we note how triangulated situations (and we'll see more of these in following chapters) create complications and a hierarchy of relationship. sister-to-sister, friend to friend. As Deborah Tannen notes in her essay, "When Friends Are Like Family," friends are considered 'family' when people are living far away or not in sync with their blood families. This was the basis for the Helen/Gabriella dyad. It was a secure and trusted stand-in for family.

Although Helen and Gabriella have moved on, Gabriella laments the absence of a long friendship and appreciates what a true friend Helen was. She tells us she is "still hoping for an explanation" for the conversations that never occurred. In contrast, Helen says she wouldn't change the relationship they shared, yet she will not reconcile. "No, it was too much," she feels. "Sometimes you have to forgive but no."

So much time has passed for Helen and Gabriella, their children are grown and by now both women's personal needs have undoubtedly shifted somewhat. Thus in a perfect world with the feelings they once shared for their friendship, one would hope they might meet again and try to make amends. Because the friendship had an unexpected ending, it is worth revisiting. This depends on both Helen and Gabriella's take on the chance of mending the friendship. What is apparent is how much meaning, commitment and care once existed and could be resurrected.

PART TWO

Toxic Bonds

CHAPTER FOUR

A Flippant Friend

> Do you respect your friend and it's not reciprocated?
>
> Is it clear that some friends are more important to her than others?
>
> Does this friend lie about her social life?
>
> Are you competing for her attention?
>
> Is the friend bossy about plans to get together?

If you have answered yes to any of these questions, you are with a flippant friend who is not treating you well or fairly:

> You and your best friend have been playing pickle ball together—it' a foursome—three days a week for the past three years. Historically you and she are partners in these games, having been besties for a decade, and the other two women are partners and longtime friends. Your friend has always been in charge and has made the schedule, getting someone from work as a replacement

if need be. That's been okay for you, it's not as if you wanted the responsibility. Six months ago your friend became a league organizer and now your game is part of that league. Your questions about this event include how she managed it, why was she secretive and what if you and the other women in the game do not want to be in the league? What is also perplexing is how the other two friends in your weekly game seemed to know about your best friend's plans and you were not informed. While your game has totally improved and you enjoy it, you are feeling bruised that all this is happening over you or away from you.

The conversations you have attempted about the issue have gone nowhere. She is breezy, bordering on dismissive. It wouldn't be politic to ask the other players in your game, they do not appear to have a problem. Everyone is enthused about what your friend has structured.

This is making you ill at ease. What you'd like is a stronger foundation with this friend—your best friend—and for her to care about your feelings in the midst of her pickleball aspirations.

In fact, she's been like this with other situations in the past and you've hung on. But where do you fit in now and how does it feel?

No Standing

Among the positive studies on female friendship, of which there are many, it is the UCLA Study on Friendship Among Women that came to mind as I wrote the composite above.

The study finds that when we respond to stress, our brain chemicals "cause us to make and maintain friendships with other women." But in my research for *Estranged* women are finding certain friendships to actually *cause* the stress. They are weighing their options as to whether or not to continue to be friends. Since we are tribal beings, we still depend on our most meaningful bonds for fortitude and safety. For that reason, when someone is cavalier or lies to us, it isn't easy to recover.

Myriad women report that in friendship, as in other aspects of our lives—work, romances, families, children—outside forces come into play. Any monumental event—a sudden illness, the death of a spouse, a tragic accident, winning a coveted award, a streak of very good or very bad luck—can affect our choices and the choices of our friends as well. Circumstances change; people change.

We understand this in a general sense, but when it comes to our closest friends, we want them to remain the same, solid and accountable. Since these friendships are so central to our lives, it's extremely upsetting when a valued friend is disloyal, thoughtless or dismissive. The friend at the receiving end can be quite shaken when this happens. Rather than taking charge and speaking with her friend about the issue, it often pushes her further away. The friendship no longer feels egalitarian. This realization rocks the very center of the friendship. After all, it is with our female friends that we have the opportunity to be fair and just. In a study by Veniegas and Peplau, the findings were that young women viewed equal-power friendships as "higher in quality than unequal friendships" (in which one member has more influence). In this inquiry I am hearing from women of every age who feel this is the case. As this applies to a **flippant friend**, there is a realization, followed by a shock value.

No Common Ground

Amy, 21, works in marketing and is in school part time in Austin, Texas. She came to realize that the closeness she felt with her 'best friend' wasn't mutual:

> I had a friend who always chose others over me. We had been close anyway, but I always knew how she felt. I wanted us to be close so I had given her the benefit of doubt for years. There were more than five times where she said it wasn't convenient to get together and it wasn't about that. She was seeing other friends and it was on social media. I cared about her, I thought of her as my best friend. Her view was to be a fun friend, not in it for anything serious. That was the conclusion that I came to. I think what was happening is that I learned what kind of friend to have, what kind of friend to keep around for good, and what a long-term reliable friend is. She just didn't see it the way I did and after a while it was too much for me.

The relationship Marla, a 62-year-old restaurant manager in Portland, Maine, had with her best friend was balanced as long as Marla did what her friend expected:

> My best friend and I walked together daily with a group. We spoke every morning and I knew I had to be there on time for her, for the walk we took. Then one day I got a call from my daughter and I had to take it. I stopped walking on the path to meet my friend and turned around. It was upsetting and I was late for her. By then she was with the group. I was still on my cell and

she screamed at me about it, truly screamed in front of everyone. It took several years for us to heal from this but it was never the same and won't ever be the same.

Dez, 61, in retail, lives in Memphis. She has two sons and four grandchildren. Personal wealth and lifestyle got in the way of a life-long friendship for her:

> I have friends since we were six and we've not been friends these last two years. This one friend in particular became absurdly wealthy and made so much money. Plus she comes from money. Over the years, she begrudged my work and when we made plans for a fancy lunch, she'd talk about her other fancy friends. She paid no attention to my life or how I had to hold onto my job. It was as if she didn't really see me or hear my story. This friend is widowed with three adult children and yet she doesn't seem to understand my life.

Dismissed

> My divorce eight years ago showed me everything about my real friends. Some of them stood with me, curious about what my custody and financial arrangement would be and a few were afraid it was contagious but stayed friendly. My closest friend sort of dropped me. She made some excuse but I knew it was about my situation. Maybe she was threatened by what I'd done. I was devastated.
>
> ROMY, 38, A HIGH SCHOOL TEACHER
> LIVING IN TAOS, NEW MEXICO

> When I made a friend through a cooking class, I felt as if I'd finally found someone who understood me. She was not a work friend, not a family friend but someone I sought out, a sister I never had. Recently, she was incredibly cruel to me. She humiliated me in front of a group of people. It was unbearable. What signs had I missed about her, who is she? Wasn't what we shared very real? I can't figure out the next steps. I'm surprised but I should know better, I'm not so young. Instead I feel clueless and hurt.
>
> RONNIE, 51, A DOCTOR, IN A SUBURBAN AREA IN THE SOUTHEAST

Replay

In *Sex Differences in Intimacy Levels in Best Friendships and Romantic Partnerships,* Pearce, Machin and Dunbar note, "two of the closest non-kin relationships that humans have are those with a romantic partner and a best friend." And an opinion piece in the *New York Times* by David Brooks asks "What Is It About Friendships That Is So Powerful?" Brooks points out that there is a "transformational power of friendship itself" since friends "get inside you."

The women in this chapter are describing the level of importance of their friends and the hardship that ensues when it doesn't work out. We're not seeing much compromise in these vignettes and the estranger seems fairly careless. But what we do see is how the women second guess, questioning how it might have worked out differently.

This reminds me of my own encounter with Paulette and how all these decades later, I still replay what happened and ask myself why it had to be so final. Recently I was going over old family photo albums with my sister-in-law. There were so many of Paulette and me, such authentic smiles, the connection evident. Over the course of this book, we'll see the back and forth that occurs as well as the finality of women's friendships. Not only the repercussions that enough women experience but the regret that it hasn't worked out. At this juncture, we are hearing apprehension in these stories. Interviewees—both estrangers and estrangees—are asking themselves: *Could it have been better, was I responsible for what happened?*

True Believers

Many of us subscribe to the idea that girlfriends come first. For example Myra, 34, a veterinarian living in southern Florida, was taught this by her mother:

> My mother, a feminist, raised me to believe that without my girlfriends I'd have very little. I have been super friendly with one woman for the past eight years. We've shared every secret possible. We are so close I haven't even needed a steady boyfriend. It's like we are a couple. I'm dreading what will happen if one of us meets someone or moves away. I bet it will blow us up.

Counter to Myra is Elise, 42, in retail, married with a son, living in Omaha, Nebraska. She has relied on her closest female friends to a fault:

> I'm always committed to my friends, that's how I am. But this one friend was manipulative and not just toward me, toward other people. Still, I wanted the closeness

and to be with her. After a long time, I've learned that it doesn't work because of who she is. I had to stop making excuses. I've learned how important it is that friends give something back too. Now I'm in a relationship and I live with someone. My girlfriend and I have been together for two years, still I want to have good female friends. The kind that won't hurt me. Today I'm better at figuring out a friendship.

These lopsided friendships have a serious impact. A study by Dainton, Zelley and Langan, finds that a ratio of outcomes to inputs needs to be equal for the level of satisfaction and friendship to work out successfully. By the time two valued friends have experienced an incendiary event, this has not been sustained. "There has to be a mutual and reciprocal trust and respect," Donna Laikind, a therapist who practices in New York City, observes. "If not, it becomes like angry siblings. The conflict between close women friends is similar to what happens between siblings because both are peers. It becomes very tense."

What is evidenced in the interviews above is the importance of getting it right as friends, and how disturbing it is when a friendship doesn't work out. Because our culture is also rife with examples of positive friendships, a failed friendship can often feel like a failure as a person. Think of the classic sitcom, *Friends*, which ran for ten years. In the show Rachel (Jennifer Aniston) and Monica (Courtney Cox) represent female friendship at its best. In Elena Ferrante's novel, *My Brilliant Friend*, Elena and Lila are tied to one another, despite ups and downs, since they were girls. They serve as each other's protection against their hometown poverty and violence.

According to Robin Dunbar in his book, *Friends: Understanding the Power of Our Most Important Relationships*, we have a kind of system among our friends. First there is a smaller group of important people, the 'tightest circle,' which consists of five people. After that, we have fifteen 'good friends,' then fifty 'friends.' When it comes to a broad sweep of people in our lives, one hundred and fifty people is the limit on 'meaningful contacts,' five hundred 'acquaintances' and one thousand five hundred are 'people you can recognize.' When we imagine our closest group of five against the backdrop of all others, it underscores how deeply held these friendships are. Even in the best of five however, there is a hierarchy. Ideal friendships have been held up to us as our goal, but in truth prove onerous to maintain.

Priorities

Consider Kaye, 34, single with two young children. She does freelance bookkeeping and lives in Marietta, Georgia:

> My best friend was supposed to be a bridesmaid in my sister's wedding. Instead, she went on vacation with her husband. Like she had no character. She could have done this right after the wedding, she could have compromised but she didn't. She said the opportunity came up last minute. I thought she could have gone another week. She didn't change her plans to be in the wedding. If she was angry with us, she could have told me. She has kids and I think it was more important to go away with them. My sister was extremely angry. Our families know each other, we grew up together. This ruined the friendship and I am upset. For me it was about how this friend didn't listen to me, it confirmed how she really is. I expected

something more. I was unheard and disrespected. She is very sorry and has tried reach out. At the moment we are not speaking. My sister does not want anything to do with her. This has changed my view of friendship. It had a negative reaction for me. And friendship has always meant so much before that.

I did accept her apology but I am not in the same space with her anymore. I see us as family friends now. I'm too injured to have our kids together. They used to hang out, but not right now. It will take time to get back to where we were, if ever. Will she listen to me and understand how I feel? That is what matters to me.

Lorraine, 41, working in sales and living in Wisconsin, also feels she has not been heard by an important friend. Nor was she invited to a family event this friend hosted:

My best friend and I are not really in the same zone. When I tell her how I feel, she isn't hearing it, she brushes it under the rug. She has not been paying attention to me as a friend. I have included her in everything I do. Then she didn't invite me and my family to her daughter's high school graduation. She did come to my son's graduation and party and then did this. She doesn't understand what is important to me. I know who was invited and that makes it worse. The problem is not just what she did but what it means. So while I hope there will be a time when we can go back to being together, we are not speaking. I feel sad, I miss her and miss talking to her.

But I'm also kind of relieved. Right now it is okay to be without her. She was a big part of my life and was there for me all the time while I was a single mother. I'm very mixed, I see both sides of it, with and without her.

Sleepwalking

Assessing what the friendship truly means to us is a wise and straightforward step. Still, we don't do it enough, as if we're not aware of the pitfalls as well as the rewards, or purposely look in the other direction.

Surely this is the case with Allegra, 23, working at a kennel, living in a small town in Maryland:

> I knew that my best friend was a materialistic person. We overlapped because of mutual friends and were thrown together before we went to separate schools. That made it easier for her to be distant. Especially when she was always looking for a better place to be, the right party to go to. She wasn't in touch because she had something better to do. I felt slighted since she'd cancel last minute with some excuse. One time she said she had a commitment at school with a professor, but she was with another friend. I was offended, I wasn't sure why she didn't tell me the truth.
>
> Things were getting more obvious. She was lying about who she was with. That's when I realized she was with people based on what they could provide for her. I learned not to trust her and our friendship came to an end. Today we are not in touch—after a series of incidents—including the time I ran into her at the gym when she said she had fever and the time she was dress shopping with another person I hardly knew.

Sometimes discovering that a friend is not who we think she is, while upsetting, can lead to much needed self-discovery. In Phoebe's narrative which follows, as in Allegra's, there is a discovery about not only the friend, but oneself. Phoebe, 53, volunteering for local charities, has three grown daughters and lives in New Hampshire:

> We had been so close, this friend and I. I can't really tell what happened. I loved her girls, she loved mine. We did so many holidays together, it was a given that we were always going to be together. She was at my children's weddings and I invited very few friends. What happened is that she changed. She had been a very good, loving friend and then it was like a switch flipped. This heavy-duty clique of women bought homes nearby. I thought it hurt our core neighborhood while she was excited. She became so involved with that crowd and there was no room for me.
>
> If I met her today, she wouldn't be my friend. It's all about fancy country clubs, queen bees, lots of drama. I don't go for judgmental or unfriendly women. How can my best friend care about this inconsequential stuff? She's living in a world that I don't want. I know it isn't worth it. She doesn't need to spell it out. I know she and I aren't like we were. I was sad but now I face it. My attitude is, if you don't want to be my friend, just leave, go.

Claiming It

By categorizing these bonds there is the assumption that friends, like family, will always remain in our lives, providing a safety net. According to a study by Cunningham and Barbee, women seek to be buoyed and buffered by their relationships with family and friends. In some cases, the stakes get higher as the friends become more connected. For the women in this chapter, when the friend's energy and care lessens or evaporates, there is little recourse but to reevaluate the friendship. How can we not take it to heart when we are dissed or excluded?

This happened with Paulette. When she had her baby naming ceremony, she told me she was not designating anyone a godmother. Yet when I arrived she announced two other friends of ours would be co-godmothers. I was not only surprised but deeply wounded. I wanted to walk out the door and it was my mother, also a guest, who advised me to stay. "Don't let her hurt you like this," she said. "Don't let her win."

Sometimes, it's an eye-opening event that wakes us up; sometimes it's an escalated series of events. In either case, once we 'own' the truth, much like a love affair gone wrong, we grieve then move on.

The anthropologist Helen Fisher explained in "The Tyranny of Love" that romantic love is evolutionary, a "universal craving," and "a drive, a survival mechanism." If we apply this concept to serious female friendships, a yearning along the same lines makes sense. When there is a serious rupture between female friends, much like between romantic partners, it is arduous. We funnel our emotions into these friendships and the level of attachment is high.

What is the truth about this friendship?

Do you find this friend placates you?

Friends who are being insincere are not always readily identifiable. Women yearn to belong and gestures by a friend who is stepping away might be confusing.

Has the friendship altered while you ignore the signs?

The old cliché, grow together or grow apart, is certainly applicable when it comes to our female friends. What if there is no attempt to hold it together?

If your friend is offhand about time and energy for you, why are you still with her?

It requires confidence to call it as it is with a female friend and then extricate yourself. We are now becoming bold enough to do it.

As the friend who is distancing, are you feeling rather guilt-free?

For women who feel they've reached their limit, there is a belief that no more energy or tolerance is required. Their need to do this outweighs guilt or self-blame.

Can you live with the psychic pain inflicted on a fraying friendship?

Women who are unhappy in a female friendship have the opportunity to soul search and better understand what they need in these relationships.

Did you ever expect to be the one who would have little left for a best friend?

For generations females have been raised to be 'good girls' and compliant. If a female friendship fails today there is a new point of view. Leavetaking is considered a viable option.

SHE SAID / SHE SAID

EXHIBIT D: Untrustworthy

Sandy and Nicole

In this next twosome, both Sandy and Nicole have yet to recover from their anger and loss. Sandy starts with an explanation of how this once treasured friendship evolved into the 'flippant friend' category. Family friends since childhood, their story is multi-layered because due to a tragedy, they became sisters as well.

Sandy

> I caught my friend/sister Nicole in her lie. She'd begun to look down on me and I know it won't ever change back. She has to have a certain kind of life and I'm too plain for her now.
>
> •
>
> Two years ago, I was coming to Little Rock on business and got in touch with Nicole who is my best friend, to visit. She said there was no chance she could move her schedule around to see me. I couldn't believe she'd say that and so after I landed and was settled, I decided to surprise Nicole anyway. That's when I found out she was having a party with all her high-end, married friends but had told me she couldn't be with me. I was shocked at her lie. We were raised together. This has hurt me beyond anything I know.

Sandy and Nicole's connection runs deep. Sandy's parents died in an accident when she was in grade school and Nicole's parents adopted and raised her. Before they became "sisters" and part of the same nuclear family, the two were best friends and their parents were best friends.

> Nicole is my distant cousin. Our parents were so close and when my parents died unexpectedly, I was left in their care. She was everything to me growing up and we needed very little, except each other. I was very close to her parents and her brothers were like my brothers. Her parents adopted me and that was the safest part of my life. Living in Nicole's house made me less sad about my own parents and the accident. Her mother and Nicole and I took cooking lessons, we read the same books. I had a lot of recovering to do about the loss and this family became my family, it helped so much. We went to the same college. We had all these secrets and dreams.

Over the past few years, since Nicole married and began to raise a family, she has distanced herself from Sandy, who had moved away:

> Nicole didn't approve that I'm not married anymore and raising a child alone. She believes I've made the wrong choice. I know what she's decided and how she's worked for the life she has for herself and her family. But we are connected in ways other best friends aren't.

Dishonesty

Sandy, 26, works as a paralegal and lives in Kansas City. As she describes her childhood, despite a terrible calamity, her experience with Nicole's parents and Nicole had been positive. Sandy feels that both she and Nicole have succeeded in their careers because they were raised with certain goals and beliefs. To this end, the situation with Nicole is acutely painful for her.

As adult women, Nicole and Sandy's personal lives and choices diverged. This applies to both love life and family, and the two friends are in different places. For Sandy, this does not constitute a deal breaker and she seems genuinely baffled by Nicole's reaction and the lie she told her:

> Ever since this happened, I've played it over and over in my mind that Nicole kept saying she was busy with her work, her marriage and her kids and then not getting back to me. There was some story about how she was too busy with her life. I ask myself if I should have stopped by like I did. I knew it was to see what the reason could be that she had no time for me. I wanted to try to be together again. What I saw was a party at her house. It was very coupled, very upscale, all her new friends. No one I knew, were there. I went inside and I was hurt and disappointed in her. I was crying because she had told me something else about why I shouldn't come to her home. There she was, hosting a big party. Why hadn't she just said the truth, that she didn't like my lifestyle and she was someone who works really hard on being married. I didn't fit in, she judged me as a single mother.

Status

From Sandy's point of view, she and Nicole were on the same page when both friends were first married and in touch frequently and living nearby. Nicole called her every day after work and it felt secure. Once Sandy's marriage fell apart, she felt Nicole was at arm's length.

> I saw Nicole was changing and not talking to me like she had. I asked her mother, who had raised me too, what was the reason. It wasn't clear to me. I thought maybe we were both just trying to build a new life and weren't living in the same place anymore. Then I realized it was that my marriage was ending while Nicole was making a life for herself with a husband. Communicating long distance changed things too. But really it was that my husband left me and it bothered Nicole. Especially since I had a two-year-old. But she never said this, she just acted it. I didn't fit in with her plan and lifestyle anymore.

When Sandy returned from her business trip, she asked their mother about it. She suggested they let it go and bury what had happened. Yet their mother was disappointed in how Nicole treated Sandy. Sandy's impression remains that Nicole did this because Sandy is not married.

> Maybe she thought I was a threat—as a single woman, and she only wanted married friends to mingle. Is that who Nicole is, someone who controls things like that? I used to trust her, but our trust was broken, I became very sad and depressed. I locked myself in the house and tried to heal. Nicole had let me down. I've known her my whole life. We had grown up together before

the accident even. After this happened, I said I wanted nothing to do with her.

Mending

Several months ago, their mother called asking that the issue be resolved. She told Sandy that Nicole's latest group of friends in her new city turned out to not be genuine friends:

> Our mother told me Nicole realized what she had done, and that these women had hurt Nicole. That I am the real friend. I said that I could forgive but not forget because when I came over that night, Nicole was so bitter and unfair to me.
>
> Today, we are becoming friends again but no more are we best friends, it's different. At least we are in touch, but it doesn't feel like sisters. We just talk, but there was a betrayal, and it never goes away. What happened with Nicole that night has changed everything. I keep thinking of what our mother said to me, "You can't leave your closest friend."

Nicole

> She wanted to see us all. I said no, I was too busy that week. I just wanted to separate from her so I lied and said there was not time.
>
> •
>
> My closest friend, Sandy, is a far distant cousin. We grew up together. She lost her parents when she was six and my parents adopted her. Our family gave her everything

and I was taught to do the same as a child. We shared the same room with twin beds, we were like sisters and we shared everything. My brothers weren't really a part of our bond, she was like a blood sister.

When we were in grade school, we swam together and were on the same field hockey team, we played games, we went to church and prayed in the morning. When we were in high school, we'd shop and watch movies. Our parents took us on vacation. Sandy loved cooking and she always helped my mom in the kitchen, so I did too. I confided in her when I couldn't tell my mother what I was up to.

Broken Bonds

Presently Nicole, 28, lives in Little Rock where she works as a data analyst. She has three young children. She recalls how she and Sandy were confidantes who supported each other:

> The only time we ever argued was when we were teenagers and I was two grades ahead. But these weren't important arguments, just the usual. I think we were sometimes competitive then, for the first time. We were both very good students and went to college together. She had a cute boyfriend and that was the first time I was jealous. She was happy, everyone was envious of them as a couple. He seemed to treat her so well.
>
> After graduation, we moved to different cities because of our work. I was married already and building a life with my husband. I saw how life changed for us because she had a child but was a single mother while

> I was married. I was someone who is respected in the community with a traditional life, children, a marriage. I have a husband who views life a certain way and so Sandy and I became distant.
>
> Then two years ago, Sandy contacted me to come visit. She said she was coming to Little Rock for her job. I said no and blamed it on work. I lied because I couldn't really be seen with her. I kept saying I was too busy. I regret that I lied and didn't say that I was uncomfortable, even in today's world, with her choice as a mother. That I had worked hard to make a place for myself and our family in this tight community. She didn't fit in or understand my life, and my married friends would notice.
>
> I stayed with the lie—that the dates she was coming to town wouldn't work."

Being outed in her lie made Nicole feel rather sleazy but she was hellbent on her new life and social crowd. This caused her to be short-sighted and the idea that Sandy would learn the truth was less a problem than having her at her party. Except that when it actually occurred, things snowballed.

> I don't know what I was thinking. Sandy learned I had a party with my friends while she was in town and did not invite her. I realized it was a mistake to treat her like that. She stopped talking to me. I texted to explain but it was too late. I had betrayed her, she said to never contact her again. It didn't matter that I knew I was wrong. I had done what I had done.

Harm and Regret

While Nicole has become reflective about the harm her actions had, the effects linger and the wounds are deep:

> For the year that we didn't speak and Sandy wouldn't respond to me, I was disappointed in myself. When my mother found out about this issue, she was very displeased. She told me that Sandy was alone with a young child, trying to take care of her life. She reminded me of how we'd grown up together and what an error it was on my part. No one bothered with my motive just the result and what it did to Sandy.
>
> A year ago I had the courage to visit her and I asked for forgiveness. That's when I saw that she was the one who understood why I did what I did. She got it. She just didn't think it was fair, given our history. We became friends again, but not the same as when we were young because I had pushed her away. I had put my new friends, who are married, first. I look back and see how it caused Sandy to sever ties.
>
> I accept what I did and I know Sandy won't trust me again. I feel so bad about it. I cry all the time, I hurt not only Sandy but what we were shown by our parents about how to treat people. To this day, in my lowest moments, I feel like my guilt will never stop, it will be with me for the rest of my life.

Can This Friendship Be Saved?

Sandy and Nicole's story is multidimensional: it is about friendship and being sisters, family and upbringing, failure and reliance. It is also clear cut—Nicole did not respect Sandy and Sandy chose to leave her as a result.

As social beings, we count on those closest to us for fortitude and safety. For that reason, when someone dear to us lies, it isn't easy to recover from the deception. Hanan Parvez's essay, "Why Betrayal of Friends Hurts so Much" addresses how humans crave intimacy yet deceit occurs due to the depth of these bonds. What is lost in an instant is the belief that this person is on your side and that what you share is valid.

Although Nicole has apologized profusely and admits to her lie, Sandy initially told her to never contact her again. Nicole acknowledges her mistake and the pain it has caused her parents as well as Sandy. For Sandy, the fact that Nicole owns up to what she did and regrets it, means something. But not enough to currently include her in her life. "What happened with Nicole has changed everything," she tells us. "I don't want any part of her anymore. She will say we are friends again, that no one understands each other like the two of us, but nothing is the same. It isn't okay at all."

What remains to be seen is if Sandy softens and forgives Nicole over time and what measures are ahead for Nicole's redemption. This particular dyad could end in estrangement or become a more superficial friendship. At the moment they are semi-estranged, while going through the motions. We'll call it 'friendship light.' Their reconciliation is for the greater good, that of their parents and their history. However what occurred is a very serious, hurtful matter.

CHAPTER FIVE

A Disparaging Friend

Does this friend find fault with you?

Is she bossy at times, like she knows best?

Are you hoping things will change?

When you are with her are you anxious?

Is it all too much to tolerate in a friendship?

If you answer yes to any of these questions, you are with a friend who makes you feel as if you are less:

> You are well aware of the instances with this friend where you have felt unsettled, although you've chosen to ignore it. For example, the time she railed against you when you invited her to an all-girls night dinner party you were hosting. Her reason was you gave her short notice and she had theatre tickets that evening. There have been other incidents such as at a lunch years ago, where you were alone together and she told you without being asked, what she thought was wrong with you. Your

hair color was faded and unbecoming, your wardrobe was outdated, you were too strict with your children, you might consider having your nose fixed and your significant other was a difficult man. You were too shaken to defend yourself and left defeated and deficient.

This friend has always accelerated the drama and been critical toward you. Your mother has made remarks about it and your other friends stay away. One of your other best friends, someone who is respectful, recently asked why you spend time with this woman. She pointed out how negative she is and how much you seem under her spell. You defended yourself, yet afterward, you decided to face how this friend makes you feel. Once you were on the west coast with her and she humiliated you in front of her two sons and your son and daughter. The rant that day was how you have taken on too much. Even on this trip she found your schedule annoying and unnecessary.

Recently there was a scene that forced you to realize how flawed this friendship is. She was supposed to pick you up to go to a lecture and had confirmed by text the day before. But she didn't swing by because you hadn't texted back and so you ended up not going. That was when you hit your limit. Maybe your mother and friends are right. You get so little from this friendship and put real effort into it. Do you know why you have stayed with her, rationalizing her actions?

Triggers

What is interesting about the **disparaging friend** is how available she is to be with you, as if torturing you is a sport. The women on the receiving end of this type of friend felt sought after. Some described it as almost an initial seduction. This makes leaving the friendship a challenge despite how undermining the friend is. Instead, the friend on the receiving end is genuinely surprised by repeated incidents of diminishment and unkindness. Interviewees tell themselves it won't happen again or it was merely an isolated incident. When there are scenes such as those described in the composite, one questions what draws the friends together and if there is a mutual attraction to the friendship.

If we compare our connections to our female friends to Robert Sternberg's Triangular Theory of Love, there are some parallels. In his study, love is divided into three parts: intimacy, passion and commitment. When it comes to our female friendships, the intimacy is about what feelings we share, the passion is about being drawn to the friend's personality and what she stands for, and the commitment is, as in romantic love, to the relationship. In this chapter, there are women who are and have been committed to the friendship although there has been inequality and mistreatment.

Why would you stay? That is the question one of my best friends asked me as I described a few narratives in this category. I explained it has to do with the depth of the friendship and wanting to hold onto the good parts despite unhappy situations. Women are adept at balancing acts. And there is always the desire to avoid defeat. Especially when it comes to the ups and downs with a friend who is disparaging. Consider the following scenarios:

> A close friend and I are hardly talking anymore. I loved spending time with her and felt compatible. Then I realized she was actually very critical and made jokes about me, mostly when we were together with other people. One on one she is fine. Then when we went on

more outings with other friends, after a while she wasn't nice.

I didn't know how to handle it. In retrospect I should have been clearer about how it felt. But I looked up to her. She is two years older and she seemed very cool when we were young. She and her family reminded me of my family and me and that made me think it was a positive friendship.

SACHA, 23, A GRADUATE STUDENT
LIVING IN THE ADIRONDACKS

When I was younger I was self conscious, and this friend knew everyone. It was okay in the beginning. After a while I saw how she got when we were with other friends. Her meanness was heightened if we were with a group. It felt like the way she spoke to me was a betrayal. It definitely lessened my trust in her. People fight back, but I wasn't confident enough about myself. We were living in the same area and introduced by mutual friends. I needed the group and I needed her. Now I know it isn't the right thing to have a friend who puts you down.

RITA, 39, A MATH TEACHER, LIVING IN UPSTATE NEW YORK

Second Chances

Women are reporting how wounded they feel when an important friend isn't fair or appreciative. Or they feel pushed away, as if the friendship is lessening. The friendship no longer feels protected and you cannot rely on your friend for integrity and assurance.

In my own case with Paulette, what proof, let alone indication, did I ever have that she was reliable or there for me? I was the one who made assumptions all along—we knew each other well, we'd gone through so many stages of our lives together since we were girls. There was absolute trust, we had each other's backs. That was the template, wasn't it? My cousin warned me after she ran into Paulette, that she had made a remark or two about me, small digs, but I didn't listen. The friendship was that central to my life.

As Janna, 30, a party planner living in northern Connecticut, views it, letting go despite what you know isn't easy:

> This friend and I met when we were fourteen. We went through all the tough years together and in our early twenties we were very involved. I was never sure how important I was to her and I knew she was more important to me. She had so many friends. There was this period of time when she made fun of me in front of people. She'd say I wasn't a good athlete or that I needed a makeover. She'd describe her other friends to me like they were amazing and it shook me up. Now I see she was the needier friend and I didn't realize it. I don't think I understood her as well as I thought I did. I decided there was no need for how she treated me. I'd hit my limit.
>
> But lately I've been thinking that maybe I can trust her again. Maybe we can't help but be in each other's lives, maybe we've matured. New friends have filled the void but I can't give so much energy to any one person anymore. Recently she asked to get together after four years without speaking.

If we compare Renee's take on a friend where there was little parity, she is less forgiving than Janna. At 43, Renee feels she has been iced by this friend. She is single and lives in a small town in New England:

> When I met this friend the first week of work, years ago, I should have ignored her. There was something uncomfortable about her. We became friends anyway. It hasn't been great and then in the past few months, she has shut me out after treating me like I wasn't worth it. I wasn't cool enough for her. First we were the only brown people in her new group. She introduced me to everyone and it was fine. Then she and this man became close. It was when everything changed. They got engaged and she wanted another kind of life.
>
> Once they got engaged I felt like she was putting me down. What I wore was dorky and she wanted to be with women who were stylish. She had liked me better when she needed me, before she met this man and got so cool. She did not invite me to her wedding, explaining I was too sensitive and wouldn't fit in. After she married this guy they bought a house where I'd grown up, right in the neighborhood. But she shut me out. I am not part of her life now.

Over thirty-five percent of my interviewees feel they've been used in some form by a friend. Twenty-five percent have reported they have felt humiliated or mistreated socially by a friend at some juncture in the friendship. Still, there is often an attachment to the friend after these strains and obstacles have set in. The question becomes, why would a woman who realizes her friend is diminishing her, stick it out? Clearly, as the recipient of this behavior, she knows she can't count on her friend or find assurance with her. Yet we do hang on, hoping for change. We don't want to let go of the productive parts of the relationship. We have become so emotionally dependent upon the friend that we don't know how to navigate life without her.

Ambivalences

An example of a friend who can neither stay nor go is Dorrie. A designer living in Boise, Idaho, at 28 she laments an ongoing complicated friendship:

> I have had so many ups and downs with this one friend. We had gone to school together and I was sure that after that we wouldn't see each other again. Which seemed fine, as long as we were friendly while we were both on campus together. It was so sickening I at times with her. She made me feel like I was always wrong, whether it came to our assignments or plans with people we knew. She would shut me out but keep me in her orbit. It was strange, but true because our other friends saw it. No one wanted to cross her or me for that matter. I would go home from college some weekends and tell my boyfriend. He had his fair share of listening to my friendship issues. I'm not sure he ever knew how to deal with my feelings. He was sorry for me but he also didn't see why I stayed with her. It's true, I was always happier away from her, with my old friends. That's why five years ago, the idea of not seeing this friend after college was fine, it could easily be that we stopped being friends once we left campus.

> During school it was confusing and stressful being friends. I'm not sorry that we met, there were definitely good times, but it was a bad scene. Really it's about how she's treated me and what she does today since I have not let go. I should and I'm working on it. I am figuring out how to leave, to stop worrying about it.

How curious that many women have remained in these less than happy friendships, as if it's all we deserve.

Consider Tabatha, 42, working for an internet company and living in western Massachusetts, who years after a clash with one friend in particular, is more mindful of who to trust:

> I have a friend who upsets me to the point where I call my mother. She always says the same thing, that it could be my fault. I'm wondering why I ask my mother since she can be insecure herself over her friends and isn't the best role model. So I decided to speak with my grandmother too. She told me to try to understand what was going on by spending more time with this friend. She said maybe she wasn't a loving person. I was uncomfortable with that idea. I mean, this friend and I were going out together. All this family advice was making it worse and more tense. I couldn't decide what to do but knew I needed to move away from her. My friend couldn't be trusted, she did too many mind games. I was confused and very shaken by it.

There are friends who are linked together despite a disparate power. Three novels where the protagonists become overly involved with their female friend come to mind. In *The Woman Upstairs* by Claire Messud, the protagonist Nora has given up a great deal in her life—children, a partner—to care for her parents. But there is her attachment to Didi, a friend, and more dramatically to Sirena, a friend/love interest. Sirena is a famous artist and Nora a minor artist who dreams of fame and this exhibits a hierarchy of friendship. We walk in Nora's shoes throughout the book, as she exemplifies what singlehood and longing are about. In *Passing* by Nella Larsen, we observe a rekindled friendship between Irene and Clare, childhood friends. Although both women are Black, Clare is married to a white man who has no idea about her background. The friends each have comfortable but very different lives. As they become more entwined, they are threatened by the truth. *The Girls* by Emma Cline is about Evie, who in the late sixties as a teenager was part of a cult. There the girls were her guides and her attachment to one female in particular, Suzanne, ran deep. In each of these novels, there is the salient theme of how frequently females submerge themselves in the friendship, miscalculating the return on the investment and what deception turns out to be. It is the allure of the friend that trips us up, even if after some time and experience, we know better.

A Path Out

Consider Liandra, 47, in banking, living in a suburb of Chicago. Her insight into what occurred with her friend is notable:

> When we were in our thirties, this friend and I were close and I wasn't paying attention. I didn't notice at first how she wanted me to be with her and we were part of the same crowd, but she couldn't leave me alone. She'd make remarks about how I looked or dressed, the hat I was wearing. I pulled away after I caught on. No scene, just quietly. Recently this friend was unhappy in her

marriage and suddenly after five years, I heard from her. I was a resource so she sought me out. She knew how to reach me and it turns out she was following me on social media. I hadn't forgotten how she disrespected me years ago. Her own husband disrespected me because she had encouraged him to look at me like she did. I was wary. I have my life and it was ages ago when we were friends and had mutual friends. I'm not mad at her, it was another era. What I am is over her. I do not want her near me and I remember how she made me feel. I pulled away and let it end.

For Finn as well, after much back and forth, there was a parting. Finn, 32, is in tech. She lives in Portland, Oregon and is single:

My life is very different since she and I are not together. It was an important friendship that grounded me and gave me a sense of belonging. The friendship was so strong that I feel unbound. I hardly remember when it wasn't that happy, when she did things that felt unfair or like I was pushed aside. Since this has fallen apart, I've tried to replace her with other, new friends. I am looking for a network now because there was too much emphasis placed on his one friend. I'm not sure I could start this again with one person after how we failed. When I think of it, I think of loss. There's no outlet for our shared experiences and there should be some special place for what we shared. We hung out in college, texting, email chains for years. After that it was messy, not very healthy, but we had each other. When I think of her now, it still hurts, I've not fully recovered from this breakup.

Divided Sisters

Before I wrap up this chapter, I'd like to include a sister story, told to us by Lora, 66, working in real estate and living in Cheyenne, Wyoming:

> My sister is seven years older than I am and always resented my birth, in my opinion. She always acted as if I were a bother and somehow inconvenient. This happened when we were children and is the same today. My childhood consisted of these times where I would try and she would turn against me and always tried to make me into less of a person.
>
> Recently, there was a wedding in the family and she traveled to our hometown. I thought this is family reunion and everything will finally be okay. I asked her to lunch and she made an excuse. Then I thought maybe a shopping excursion or going hiking together might work, but again she wasn't available.
>
> I have always been the good daughter almost to fill her shoes. My older sister separated from this family a long time ago. We have a younger sister and a younger brother, but they are not part of the problem. They don't know her as well as I do because she moved away when she was in college. But moving away wasn't enough. She wanted to cause harm and has been mean to all of us. To me, she has been especially nasty. She has two daughters and I have two daughters but they never see each other despite all my efforts. And our mother, when she was younger wanted more than anything for us to be close.
>
> The truth is my older sister never cared. She found me annoying, and someone who was in her way. Our father was a judge in our hometown and there was respect for

our family. She always had secrets and my mother was always covering up for her. One time she was arrested for drunk driving. I remember how this was for my parents. They were shaken and embarrassed.

My other sister and brother have always been proud of our father and mother. She never respected them and over time she'd do cruel things. In public she would act strange and it was wrong, she knew it was wrong. After that, she just turned against them.

We have not spoken in five years and live in different parts of the country. I am tired of trying, but I always wanted to have a good relationship with her and now in midlife I realize it was never possible. I don't want to blame anyone, but I do think it's about her. There were these scenes when I was growing up, between my mother, my aunt and my sister.

Today my sister is remarried and has moved to Seattle. I have stopped reaching out to her, based on comments she's made, it's clear that she looks down on how I raised my children and how I live my life.

I've finally stopped searching for something that doesn't exist. It has taking me so long to understand all of this. Sometimes when I hear about sisters and they are so close, I feel I really missed out. I have very good women friends and that helps, but what matters is what I've learned. I can separate myself and accept that we'll never have the kind of sister relationship I wanted.

Recognition

If one person in a dyad is critical and unfair, in any relationship, the other person feels crestfallen. The friend who is deprecating spawns an infective environment, as shown to us in this section. Finn's story above has an almost amorous element, she is accepting but almost flattened by what transpired. As I mentioned in the beginning pages of this book, women are better at ending romantic relationships than complicated female friendships. Through nonfiction books, articles, streaming, film, novels about being in the throes of a romantic relationship, we are shown how to fix things. These are expected experiences, rites of passage. If we apply this to Lora's relationship with her sister, after high hopes for years, it is only when she is honest with herself that she is set free.

While some interviewees are willing to consider reconciliation or one more chance at mending a friendship, others are not. At this juncture, we realize how women get by. The obvious choices in this book are: 1) embracing healthy female friendships (the goal), 2) enduring the rocky friendships (we've seen this threaded throughout), 3) in a changing culture, at last having the ability to face a very flawed friendship. In this mode, we come to a path where estrangement is often the solution.

Let's consider the following questions.

Is it true you know your friend's personality but feign she isn't like that?

In enough instances we tell ourselves our friend is how we imagine she should be, not as she actually is. This only leads to disappointment and distance.

If you know the friendship is disappointing, why have you hung onto it?

The idea of fixing a friendship is appealing, especially if you are family friends or have been together for years. Women will work at making the friendship more meaningful than it is.

If your friend puts you down or separates from you, does it feel like defeat?

Women who have clarity and confidence can count their losses and move on. A constructive approach is to not blame themselves, rather to own what is happening.

Are you the one who leaves, despite what it can do to your best friend?

The estranger who leaves doesn't usually dwell on what it does to the estrangee. She has thought carefully about parting.

But if you regret your decision, do you imagine a way back to the friend?

It isn't easy to re-enter a friendship where you instigated the leave-taking. It creates mixed messages and inflicts another round of pain on the friend.

Do you rationalize what this friendship was about—viewing it as less or more than it actually was?

An honest assessment of who the friend was and wasn't often helps both the estranger and the estrangee. If we are truthful with ourselves about an estrangement, it justifies the decision.

SHE SAID / SHE SAID

EXHIBIT E: Secrets Spilled

Sarah and May Lynn

In this two-sided tale of bad faith and poor judgment, we realize how apologies and remorse can prove insufficient. Sarah and May Lynn's friendship is squandered and both parties are severely affected. Let's start with Sarah's story.

Sarah

> When I heard there would be a DNA test, I knew May Lynn's life might be ruined.
>
> •
>
> My best friend, May Lynn, was getting married. She is three years older and our mothers have always been friends. Our families are very friendly too and she has always been in my life. We grew up together and used to hang out all the time. Whenever we went we had fun. We did random things and we'd go shopping or to the movies. We had this history of arguing, nothing serious but minor disagreements. We'd settle the issue the same day. We were there for each other.

Today Sarah carries the burden of how their friendship disintegrated and her part in the process:

> May Lynn and I were roommates right after college. All that we wanted was for both of us do well. That meant our work, our other friends and the men we were dating.
>   We weren't competitive. Really we wanted what was best for each other.

The Reveal

Sarah, 30, lives in St. Louis where she is a high school teacher. She is married and has a very young daughter. Today she and May Lynn are not in contact. As such close friends from the same background and raised similarly, they trusted one another with their secrets. They spoke or saw one another daily and never doubted their friendship.

> This secret ruined everything. May Lynn told me what was going on, that was the start of it. A month before the wedding May Lynn got pregnant and she confided in me that the child was not her fiance's. She said it had been a one-night stand and no one else could ever know. Her fiancé believed this was his child and she wanted it like that. Once they were married and he was her husband, she kept it going, her husband believed the child was his. No one else was told the truth, May Lynn told me because we were best friends for our whole lives. Once she was married we saw each other three times a week.
>   I never told anyone. Then one night I was drinking and I blurted it out to friends—my friends and May Lynn's friends because we share friends—that this baby was not May Lynn's husband's. The next day May Lynn got in touch with me to say someone who was there—one of our mutual friends—had told her what I did. Once May Lynn's

husband heard, he said there had to be a DNA test for him and the baby. There was the testing and it turned out as I said it was and that broke up her marriage. Her husband filed for divorce. I drank too much, that's what happened. May Lynn said that she will never ever forgive me and that I ended her marriage and ruined everything.

Amends

Not only was May Lynn's mother very angry with Sarah but her own mother was also extremely upset with her. Her mother chastised her, stating she should not have said what she said. Both mothers felt that Sarah betrayed May Lynn and their families. The fallout extends to the friendship the mothers shared. Both families have disengaged along with May Lynn's decision to separate from Sarah.

Sarah has made gestures toward May Lynn—reaching out to her via text, calls, emails and through mutual friends. She has admitted to her guilt and shame, however, there is no recovering the friendship or family bond:

> I've run into May Lynn and have tried to say hi. She has ignored me. We have mutual friends and they know both sides. A few have tried to get us together and it has gone nowhere. Other friends know to stay away from a bad situation.
>
> I feel terrible. I did the wrong thing. I said I was sorry, I tried talking to May Lynn but she refuses to speak with me. It is with me every day. My husband said what I did was very wrong and a big mistake.
>
> I think about it all the time, I still feel bad and maybe I always will.

May Lynn

> We had been friends for ages, most of our lives and we really trusted each other. So I told Sarah my secret and she promised to never tell a soul.

•

> My mother showed me how my best girl friends were so important. I come from a warm and kind family. My mother's best friend was Sarah's mother and she and I were raised to be the same. For most of my life we were together, Sarah and I were with our mothers when we were young, the four of us for all the mother/daughter things. Later Sarah and I were together like best friends are. Everything was fine and we were happy. I had no idea I couldn't trust Sarah and that she didn't care about my life. I see her as someone who is a double dealer.

Duplicity

Currently not married, May Lynn, 33, lives in St. Louis where she works in a bookstore. As a single mother to a young daughter she is devastated by the outcome of Sarah having exposed her secret:

> Sarah betrayed me. Three years ago, right before I got married, I had this fling. I should not have done it and I know that. But I did. I decided to not tell my husband, it was a one-night stand and it would only have upset him. I did confide in Sarah and she promised to never tell a soul. Then, one night she was drunk and she told our friends and ruined my marriage. She announced this wasn't my husband's baby. It wasn't her secret to tell,

it was mine. I could blame it on the drinking but it is also what Sarah did.

When my husband found out and insisted on DNA testing, it was a problem. My world was falling apart and the DNA tests were scary. I was very afraid because I could see how it could upend the life I had. When the results came in he decided he wanted a divorce. I was very surprised that my husband would not stay with me and said it was over. I know what I did is bad but we could have had a nice life together. I was furious with Sarah. How could she do this to me?

Beyond Repair

Once Sarah announced the truth about May Lynn's child's father, she became a disparaging friend, one who has no regard for her friend's secrets or how deeply she has harmed her. The trust is irreparably damaged:

> It is very complicated for me because I have my daughter. I remember daily how it would have been fine but Sarah ruined my life. I am supporting myself and when Sarah offered to help me financially, I turned her down. I am so angry with her.
>
> I never wanted to hear from her again and I wanted nothing to do with her. She apologized and I know she made a big mistake. I know it wasn't on purpose but it was a big careless mistake that cost me my marriage. I know she is sorry but I feel the way I feel. We were such great friends. Sarah was at my wedding and then this.
>
> Today I have nothing to do with my ex and that is very

upsetting too. I actually truly loved him and I am so sad about the situation. My daughter is three and it would be great if he would see her but he won't. He and I have mutual friends plus friends of friends in common, just like Sarah and I have mutual friends. So everywhere I go I see someone who reminds me of what happened.

As of today, May Lynn has no intention of communicating with Sarah again. She feels that this experience has forever changed her view of female friendship:

We were very close and shared everything. We never had a problem of any kind before this. The thing is, I only told one person my secret and that was Sarah. She was so careless. I doubt even in the future I'll ever be with her again. I know we can never be friendly. I lost the life I wanted because of Sarah. I do not believe that I can ever trust anyone again, never a female friend. I have talked to my mother who told me that despite that what Sarah did seems unforgivable, she and I have been friends since we were small. I have to find a place in my heart to forgive her so I can move on.

I cannot find that place. What I do know is if I ever find love again, I'd marry still. I would welcome the support and the relationship. I do wish I had someone. It is not easy to support myself and my daughter. Here I am, single with a child thanks to Sarah and there she is married with a child. It isn't fair, it should not have been like this. Now it's about caring for myself.

Can This Friendship Be Saved?

As we realized with another entangled family friendship—that of Sandy and Nicole in the previous chapter—complications arise. Since the friendship is multi-layered and generational—mothers and daughters, mutual friends—trust and loyalty existed, they were a given. For May Lynn, it is as if the foundation of her life is gone. While she has lost the most, this is a tale of two betrayals. First May Lynn betrayed her husband (fiancé at the time) and then Sarah betrayed May Lynn's confidence.

Suzanne Degges-White Ph.D. writes in *Psychology Today*, "When Friends Reveal Secrets You've Asked Them to Keep," there is a "rule about ethically-inspired relationship agreements." Because trust is earned, she points out, one must be respectful and keep her promises. In Sarah and May Lynn's situation, when Sarah revealed May Lynn's secret the results were staggering. May Lynn's life is shattered, as is their friendship. Diana Nash, a grief expert, notes we must distinguish between mourning for a deceased friend versus a close friend who is no longer in one's life.

"If the person is gone because she's dead, she is physically gone. When it has to do with a relationship, it can be worse because the person is gone from your life but still walking around," she tells us.

CHAPTER SIX

A Green-Eyed Friend

> Are you hesitant to tell this friend your good news for fear she'll sabotage it?
>
> Is she competitive rather than supportive?
>
> Does she constantly compare her success to yours?
>
> Has she ever said negative things about you to mutual friends?
>
> Is it possible she wishes you ill but wants the friendship?

If your friend is capable of any of this, you are with a friend who hardly contains her jealousy toward you.

> You and this particular friend have always, since high school, been in the same group. Through every phase of your lives, five of you have been together. In theory, it should be a love fest: experiences are shared, you are a team, rallying for each other. And it's true, except for this one friend. She has been competitive toward you from the start, bordering on rivalrous or jealous. When you

were crowned homecoming queen, she acted strangely. While everyone else in the group was genuinely excited, she held back. She said to you when you were alone for a moment, "I wonder why you won." She was the first of the group to get married, but you had a baby before anyone else. In fact, she immediately became pregnant when you announced that you were. Each of her three daughters is six months younger than your three sons.

Although it's fortunate that you and she are not in the same industry, she acts like you are. When you changed companies, she had to do the same. Of course with such different careers, there's no reason to compare salaries, yet she tries to. What's so disquieting is how no matter what she has—and she's fortunate—it isn't enough when it applies to your life.

Recently there has been some good news at your end. Your son received a scholarship to his first-choice college. Next you received an award at work then you won a cake-off that you entered just for fun. While everyone else in the group was enthused, she was lukewarm. Wasn't it obvious to your mutual friends that she's been mean spirited toward you? If anyone else sees it, which you know is the case, everyone has decided on an oath of silence. You're beginning to wonder why no one has defended you and why this friend has singled you out. You can't leave the group to escape her—those are your closest friends too, not only hers. Time goes on and she continues to control things. And you feel unable to find any recourse or a way out without it being your loss. Beyond that, you don't understand why this friend is so jealous.

Obvious Signs

The composite above underscores how important it is for women to belong and how negative energy from one friend is stressful and damaging. It also underscores the fallout from an unsupportive, rivalrous friend. It isn't that women aren't competitive, envious or jealous at some point in their lives. Most of us have felt pangs of jealousy toward a friend when she announces her great news, although we sincerely wish her well. So while female rivalry exists, in this chapter, I am focusing on how we deal with a friend whose jealousy harms the targeted friend and the group at large.

In a study *Our Grandmothers' Legacy: Challenges Faced by Female Ancestors Leave Traces in Modern Women's Same-Sex Relationships*, Tania A. Reynolds found that there is a contradiction in women not liking competition while simultaneously showing signs of rivalry with one another. She notes that as married women they avoided "competitive and status-striving peers, instead preferring kind, humble and loyal allies." We've seen the dichotomy in our own lives and in contemporary culture. Three films that come to mind are *Bride Wars, Barb and Star,* and *Barbie*. Each is about a certain provocation that affects female friendships.

In *Bride Wars* two best friends are put to the test when they vie for the perfect wedding and must have the same date at the Plaza Hotel. Anne Hathaway and Kate Hudson as childhood besties show us how easily the dark side of female competition can rise to the surface. In *Barb and Star*, two best friends played by Kristin Wiig and Annie Mumolo, find themselves in over their heads on a trip to south Florida. This triggers all sorts of unexpected behavior, with Star accusing Barb of being jealous of her. And in *Barbie* we watch the many Barbies with their impressive careers, happily ensconced in matriarchal Barbieland. In this place where men do little, Ken is bored and vapid, while female solidarity increases. It is when Barbie, played by Margot Robbie, enters the real world that she is exposed to sexism and patriarchy. This is where she endures the hardships that arise.

Celebrity rivalries are frequently in the news, including the *Us Weekly* reveal of a falling out between Madonna and Gwyneth Paltrow. In *Marie Claire's* piece, "32 of the Most Legendary Hollywood Rivalries" there is mention of great tension between Olivia Wilde and Florence Pugh during the production of *Don't Worry Darling*. Another mention is that Lauren Conrad and Heidi Montag had gone from "BFFs to rivals."

Women in real life can be jealous of other women over the 'rewards'—what we are encouraged to desire in contemporary society—beauty, success, partners/husbands, children, a material life, popularity. I'm also hearing of friends who are jealous that their mutual friends are spending time together without including them. It is worth considering the level of jealousy found with a **green-eyed friend** and what this yields. For example Rachel, 49, an interior designer and mother of three living in Chicago, is conscious of her feelings about her lifestyle versus her friends' lifestyles.

> It took me a long while to stop thinking that every one of my friends had more. Once my career took off and then I married a good guy, I relaxed a little. But the children, all four of mine, became another reason to compete. Around here everyone compares themselves and their kids and what they have. I finally got too busy at work and trying to be a good mother to keep up the competition. I don't want my kids, especially my girls, to fall into the trap where you're jealous of your friends.

In contrast is Darcy, 44, who feels she suffered from her friend's jealousy. Darcy works in sales for a start-up and lives in Oregon:

> My friend reached out after eight years of not speaking. She sees I've done well and I have something she'd like to have. She followed my progress and decided I'm worth pursuing. She was always transactional. She asked if my parents would sell her their house. Everything of mine she wanted, she wanted to buy the house to win. It is all about herself, her agenda. She had stopped speaking with me originally and didn't let our mutual friends stay in touch with me. She twisted it so that these mutual friends were never equal friends and they were her friends first. They had to favor her. She controlled it all. Always she had to be competitive and could not just let things be. She was always jealous of me.

Jealous but Bonded

Over the course of this book we see repeatedly how enticing it is to synchronize with a friend. This applies to each category of friendship in my study. However for the kind of friend who covets what her friend has, group friendships work well. They provide a rich environment for women to pair up and still be part of something larger. When we contemplate a bevy of females, from as early as fifth grade to women in their eighties, there is a great emphasis placed on belonging—and this occurs with all types of friends. We congregate for the right reasons: camaraderie, to be understood, appreciated and to mirror each other's goals and aspirations.

Based on my interviewee pool, many women are eager to be immersed in a circle of friends and no individual wants to rock the boat. Thus the one friend who operates covertly as a jealous friend targets the person who is the object of her feelings. Unfortunately that friend is put in a difficult situation. Even if her other friends in the group watch what is going on, no one will take action. They can't afford to lose their place and so they tolerate bad behavior as long as it's not directed toward them. Several women in this chapter describe these cases. There is trepidation around getting together with the coterie of friends and pressure to pretend all is well.

What adds to the fray is that female rivalry is still not a topic many women want to address. Although we've all been exposed to different degrees, the very idea that a friend could root for our failure so that she could seem more successful is chilling. For the person who knows her best friend can be jealous, there is rarely the shield that accompanies wholesome female friendships. An example would be Gemmy, 20, presently a student at a Midwestern university, studying nursing:

> I met this friend in college. We were hanging out for a time and doing everything together. We were from the same background. It was something we shared along with this group of friends. I had a boyfriend first, before anyone else and that upset my friend. Why wasn't she happy for me? Instead she was jealous. I once witnessed where this friend and another friend were having a conversation. My friend was crying, accusing the other friend of not liking her anymore. I decided I had to remove myself and I became colder. I wanted to avoid conflict but I did tell her my self-esteem was impacted by what was going on. She was annoyed at me and that I still had a boyfriend. I doubt she knew she had an effect

on me. It was a stressful situation. There is a lot we don't say and we do things that hurt each other's feelings. Mostly she starts it, and it always comes back to my boyfriend. She can't stand it. The other problem is when I see our shared friend she gets angry. She acts like I'm her territory. But this other friend is a better person for me and we get along well. The first friend resents we are close and that she brought me into the group. I know I need to move away from this friend and all her rivalry.

Jealous by Nature

The takeaway is that when females have more agency and it is a level playing field, the jealousy quotient will be reduced. There won't be vying for the limited goods, we can be open with our feelings, understanding where they come from. Then, in theory, females, from grade school onward, will have less need to be jealous of each other. Or so it should be, in a perfect world. Except it isn't that facile and jealousy is demanding. When I wrote my book/study *Tripping the Prom Queen: The Truth about Women and Rivalry,* I identified female rivalry as consisting of three parts: competition, envy and jealousy. I reported that competition is "I'm willing to fight you for what I want," envy is "I want what you have" and jealousy is "You've got something I want—and I want you dead"—or at least out of the picture.

In my ongoing research, these definitions hold up and women today find themselves placed in rivalrous positions—at work, socially, in family hierarchies, when it comes to romance and friendship. Yet at the same time, few of us want to get involved or take sides, the status quo is important to everyone. The goal is to avoid anything negative and so jealousies fester without being addressed. Consider: Laila, 40, who lives in North Carolina, where she works as a teacher. She laments the loss of a friend even though she viewed her as someone with 'bad vibes' and a social climber.

> My best friend for twenty years and I had a fight over a condolence call. It was during Covid and a family member had died. She wouldn't come to the funeral because she was avoiding a crowd. She wouldn't even pay a condolence call where she could have worn a mask and just stopped by. This friend and I belong to a tight group of friends and that matters to me. Everyone had always thought of this one friend as selfish. What happened here wasn't right. Especially since if it had been the wealthy friend in our group who had invited her she would have done it. She would have been too worried about not showing up.
>
> She's jealous of this person who now has money. But she wants to be her friend, that's the other side. All the while she's crazy that our friend has this elegant life.
> I think she is jealous of me too, my daughter, my husband. She's a jealous person but I'm not the one who stopped being her friend. I must have said something to her about how she operates. Now she's stopped talking to me. Since then I've made many different kinds of friends. I have antennae for the wrong friend now.

There's no question that Laila is entrenched with her cluster of friends and not happy with her friend who seems opportunistic. If we contemplate Avery's experience, she admits to being less than thrilled by her best friend's good fortune. At 53, she lives on Long Island and works in the shoe business. She is a single mother with two grown children.

There is one woman who is my age. She's part of our friend circle and her life just changed. What's strange is that she was not doing well. She was divorced from some deadbeat husband for a long time. I'd give her my kids' old clothes. She was working day and night. Everyone in our friend group felt terrible for her. Then her son got a scholarship for an ivy league college and she met a man, a widower, online. They got married. Everyone was shocked at how this happened so fast. They had this amazing wedding and she moved into a beautiful house. I hoped to stay friends. I thought she might know someone for me. Meanwhile, I wished I had met this man online. My friend knew how I felt, how I was struggling with my own kids getting student loans and I'm alone. She went from sympathetic to out of the picture. The group began to fall apart after that and she is in her husband's world, not ours. I'd been a loyal friend and it was very hurtful when she bailed on us. At the same time, I'm asking myself how she pulled this off.

Idolspizing

A blended word, Idolspizing is to idolize + despise at once. Meaning you idolize someone and at the same time detest the person, as in despise. I investigated this in my book *Toxic Friends* and placed this type of action in the chapter titled "Intimate Frenemies." When it comes to female bonds, it is totally possible to have these opposing feelings. Idolspizing can apply to a green-eyed friend. After all, she is your friend, you spend time together and in many cases you have a shared history, yet her jealousy—or yours—is palpable.

Dr. Donald Cohen, a therapist tells us "Females are competitive by nature. It has always been there and when a friend is very appealing and popular, it stirs up envy and jealousy along with admiration. That isn't to say the friends do not remain friends. They might or might not, depending on how smoothly things go."

Consider Marci, who at 36 looks back on a roommate who was always sending mixed messages. Today Marci, located in a southeastern city, has two small sons and is a yoga instructor. This friend lives thousands of miles away:

> In college I had a roommate who I liked but I think she was jealous of my looks and my popularity. I was always invited to parties and I was hipper. My mother pointed out how this friend was—totally jealous but also wanted to be my friend. I understood, although I didn't want it to be so. We did a lot together and got along well. She was vain and always wanting to look just right. One night she attempted suicide. I found her and took her to the ER. I stayed with her and called her parents. I tried to help her in every way. Afterward her father came to school and my roommate and her father accused me of starting a rumor about her on campus. They were actually passing the rumors and treated me badly. I was upset and felt alone. She had a few friends who helped strew this around. My roommate seemed happy that I somehow had this problem. Other times she just seemed jealous, I could feel it. When I asked her to help stop this talk about me that was untrue she wouldn't. What she did was keep the accusations going.
>
> A few years later this roommate wanted to come visit me and I'd moved to Atlanta. She said she'd stay for three days and then stayed for many more days. The last night

she was with her friends and didn't invite me to join her. I was getting that jealous vibe again and when she left, I decided I wanted nothing more to do with her. We have not spoken since.

For Jamie, 45, single, living in Buffalo where she is an expert in ecology, it has been a long road with an idolspizing friend.

I come from a female oriented family with lots of women figures. I grew up with my mother and grandmother and older sister all being very independent. Later, when my best friend and I were teenagers, we'd go off with boys. I was like a boyfriend substitute for her once her life fell apart. We'd known each other since we were ten years old in a normal way. But then her father was sent to prison and it changed her and everything for her and her family. We stayed friends but she was out there. She would date two men at once and switch from one to another. She manipulated people, including me. What she wanted was my stable upbringing, my stable life. She was always predatory, always competitive. Eventually she saw my world was a material one and she wanted it. She cared about me and respected me. At the same time hated me and was jealous of what I had. I stayed in our friendship for years, pretending she wasn't like that. She was so methodical about her goals and her actions. I knew I had to break free of that, I had to get myself back. Finally about ten years ago, I did.

Helen Whitaker in her essay "Is Competition in Female Friendship The Last Taboo?" writes "There's a messy middle ground that exists between encouragement and envy, where you can simultaneously want the best for someone, while also wanting slightly better for yourself."

This reminds me of Paulette, who years after being in my my wedding was still sending mixed messages. When I made my announcement that I was pregnant for the first time and she was still single, she was quite lukewarm. I remember how she nodded her head and looked away. There were no questions about it, the usual ones—what a best friend would ask: when was the baby due, did I have any names in mind, hopes for a girl or a boy. Rather it wasn't of interest to her. *She's just jealous, our mutual friend said, why do you bother with her?*

Competitive Sisters

For the sister narrative, let's consider Riley, 29, who tutors grade school children in Minnesota. Although she and her sisters have always been very connected, her sister's treatment of a friend in common came as a surprise:

> I have always been close with my three sisters and trusted their judgment. But one day I was walking with my oldest sister and we met a lady who was a bit chubby. My sister said something negative and shamed her. I tried correcting her and afterward I noticed she didn't feel sorry. Not at all. I tried to say something to her but she said I was trying to be morally correct. Next we ran into a friend on the path who is very successful and pretty. My sister again said something negative afterward.
>
> Since my sister isn't usually like that, or so I thought, I was surprised. I had no idea she could be vicious, I was unnerved by it. We're all from the same background and my sister should know better. When we went home my

sister wouldn't listen to how I felt. She said I was always correcting her. She seemed almost bitter toward the second woman we'd met while we were outside. That's when I realized my sister could be competitive with other women and judgmental. It also made me think she hadn't been that nice to me over the years, maybe she was competitive with me too. I explained how I felt and she said I didn't understand her, that was her defense. But it put me on guard.

After that I pulled back, I didn't want to communicate with her and watch her make fun of everyone. With her view of me—that I was worth envying—I decided I'm better off with friends. These would be friends that I chose, not because we are sisters. I did the right thing to stay away but I miss this sister. We had spent so much time together. I haven't really been with her in a year.

Belonging

Despite what I've documented above, there's also an assumption that females tend to be more cooperative than competitive. This is an ideal rather than a reality in many cases. In an abstract by Kuhn and Villeval, "Are Women More Attracted to Cooperation Than Men?" the authors found that women are more likely to choose "team-based compensation than are men." Another part of their study found a tendency for women to be more generous in the "dictator game." This means women would prefer cooperation and openness. To this effect, possibly women in larger groups have a different attitude and the ratio of collaborative to covetous differs as well.

Within this framework of female organizations, GFWC/General Federation of Women's Clubs caught my attention.

This association has a presence in every state with a mission of being "dedicated to community improvement by enhancing the lives of others through volunteer service." In interviewing several presidents of GFWC, I learned of their commitments and social networking. Members (with some of the smaller clubs consisting of thirty to others having more than one hundred) range in age from 25 to 98, including a diverse group of women—working mothers, daughters, widows, single women, sisters. There are fundraisers supporting causes including food banks, women in STEM, human trafficking, domestic violence awareness and prevention and medical support. Community service, arts and culture, education, libraries and environmental issues are a part of the GFWC. The overall atmosphere according to presidents and past presidents is one of respect, support and encouragement.

When I asked about breakout groups that focus on a specific 'assignment,' one president stated that there have been incidents with 'differing points of view.' She explained it wasn't rivalry per se but more a reflection of how women interact. Another president pointed out that women join for different reasons, some for what they can get out of it and others for what they can give. There is occasional friction over expectations or when women are looking for social connections rather than community service. What prevails is a sense of belonging. Long-standing friendships flourish within this system and there is pride in the volunteerism.

If we circle back to what women search for in their female friendships, belonging and being known and truly understood are the constants.

Consider Mira, 51, who has been involved in women's organizations her entire life. She works in eldercare, lives in Wyoming and has a college age daughter:

> We might pretend it's perfect to do charity work with other women, but it isn't. I have been a member of the women's auxiliary at my church and part of a working women's network for years. These women are my closest friends but one of them isn't that nice. I've always looked the other way. No one at these meetings wants any part of what goes on with this friend. But now I'm feeling like I've had it. She said things in front of everyone when I told her that my daughter had landed a great job. "If my daughter was in the same field as I'm in, I could pull off the same," was her response. It wasn't kind or correct and the entire room heard. Maybe she wishes it had been her daughter not mine. That's the day I decided enough. I stopped being friends with her. It's better although I never thought I could manage it.

Although this friendship was within a circle of friends, Mira was able to become the estranger to her green-eyed friend, the estrangee. This shows us that a woman will eventually leave the group if she has the conviction to end the friendship and her self preservation is at stake.

In this chapter there are salient questions to be addressed.

Have you hidden behind other friends to avoid the issues with this friend?

The more intimidating the friend, the less likely we are to extricate ourselves. If you face your fears, it will help to take necessary steps.

Do you believe that immersing yourself in group activities lessens the concerns with this one particular friend?

As we have seen, being part of a coterie of women is appealing. But there is a lingering effect in dealing with a jealous friend.

Are you able to imagine life on the other side of this friendship?

If you are imagining happiness without this friend, it is time to put it into play.

Has it become apparent to you over time that your friend covets what you have?

If your friend has put you through the ringer with her jealousy and you've sensed it for a long while, it is time to rethink things.

Would you agree that you have been in denial and now are stronger?

Being strong enough to leave a friend whose life is connected to yours is a big leap. And a form of self-honesty.

Do you have the courage to risk losing the group to be free of this friend?

If you have the courage to stand up to your friend and break away, you also know that her jealousy will follow you. The tradeoff is your freedom.

SHE SAID / SHE SAID
EXHIBIT F: Double Betrayal

Beatrice and Joy
Madison and Cate

For this chapter, I'll focus on Beatrice and her daughter Madison as they report what happened with Joy and her daughter Cate. Beatrice, 51, and Madison, 22, describe this four-way connection as very close. Until this mother/daughter friendship became a double dose of green-eyed friends.

Beatrice

> When I stopped speaking to Joy, her daughter froze my daughter out. She was banished for three years.
>
> •
>
> Joy and I were best friends and out daughters were best friends since they were toddlers. But I knew that both of them were jealous of us as the years went on. When we were on the volleyball team and travelled to Nevada, her daughter got the other girls to all gang up against my daughter. Joy promised to stop the situation, but she didn't. Instead once we got home, her daughter kept it going, she froze my daughter out. Madison was banished by Cate for three years. To this day, I remember this shouting match that began the minute Joy and I brought

our girls into the gym. We'd travelled all the way from Long Island with the team and some of the girls didn't even have enough money to go or their families didn't want them to go. There was supposed to be a team spirit and instead it was just craziness. Joy and I were the two mothers in charge.

Balking

Today Beatrice lives in Douglaston, New York, and is a guidance counselor. She is married with two daughters. From the start of the trip to Las Vegas, she questioned if it was the right decision. What was intended as a bonding trip for the entire team felt instead like a competition—who was on Cate's side and who chose Madison. In retrospect, she is uncertain what the fight was about but concedes the two daughters had been competitive with each other:

> We were a long way from home and the trip was supposed to be about the girls connecting with other teams and making new friends. Both Joy and I were going to be the accompanying mothers. It was a good idea and good for our daughters who were best friends, so that part seemed fine. But at the airport, the girls began to fight and once we arrived it was worse. The girls did not get along at all. Joy and I decided that Cate would apologize to Madison. Instead it just escalated. What upset me was that both the girls and Joy and I were all fighting. It was a big mess. They said they'd talk about it the next day and they never did. It didn't feel right and there was all this tension between our two daughters and then between us. The other girls seemed confused

because they expected mostly to play and then for us to take them around the area. Instead the other girls began to take sides, deciding would they support Madison or Cate. Joy and I were watching our daughters have this major blowout. Again I told Joy it had to stop and she defended Cate. I became really upset and told her it was Cate who instigated other girls to gang up on Madison. The other two mothers who had travelled with us were quiet but I could tell they were not pleased and thought what was going on was wrong. It made me feel uneasy, like they understood Joy's take on things more than mine.

What was worse was that Joy and I were so defensive about our daughters that we couldn't act mature. I look back on it now and although Joy and I called ourselves best friends, we had a rocky history since the girls were small. Wasn't that why we couldn't stop them from this drag out fight? She seemed angry at me, probably it had been simmering for years. I began to wonder if Joy and I had ever been solid friends, the kind you trust no matter what.

Their daughters' very public fight made Beatrice anxious. Although Joy promised, she did not ask her daughter to make amends. When Beatrice realized this she wondered if Joy had influenced Cate to behave this way toward Madison:

> Finally it was so awful that Madison and I decided we would fly home early. I felt terrible because I knew Madison wanted to be in the games. But she was too bruised and upset by Cate and how the other girls listened to her. If we flew home we'd get out of the environment. I thought it was for the best. I checked with Joy who agreed it would ease the tension and the girls

would be better once everyone was back home. But after we left, everyone turned against us for not toughing it out. Things got worse.

The Return

As I have noted in my research on mothers and daughters and in my book/study *You're Grounded Forever but First Let's Go Shopping*, a mother's influence has great impact in how her daughters relate to their peers and their view of life. This certainly was the case when Beatrice in defense of her daughter and for own sake, returned early from Las Vegas. However, once the team was back, none of the mothers spoke to Beatrice and Madison was pushed out of the 'right table' in the lunchroom. Joy claimed Beatrice's exit with her daughter was the wrong message to the group, while Beatrice insisted she and her daughter were deceived and that she had cleared the plan with Joy:

> I began to wonder if Joy and I were imploding because of our girls' behavior in Las Vegas or if we were like this because our friendship was tanking. Whatever I did with my family Joy resented. She knew how close I was with my girls and that I had high hopes for them. I wanted them to be good students and to have good friends and live a solid life. Joy seemed to resent this and had somehow taught Cate to feel the same.
> What bothered me most was not only how I felt about not being on good terms with Joy but what it was doing to Madison in school. I had to put so much energy into this that I also worried it wasn't fair to my other daughter who was three years younger. It was like Joy and I were

at war. All those Sunday night dinners together were gone, all our time with our girls was over.

Self Doubt

Beatrice noticed she was becoming short-tempered with her own daughters because she felt so fraught over the mother/daughter feud. She began to wonder who she could trust in their hometown:

> This became a hard time for me. I kept asking myself the same questions over and over. Why didn't Joy want her daughter to make it right? When we first moved to Douglaston our girls were toddlers and played together constantly. That's why I gave her the benefit of the doubt when this happened. It was the kind of friendship where we spent a lot of time together. Then the tension began, Joy made me feel like she had perfect kids and my girls were the problem. There was constant competition over sports and parties and popularity. My girls were into sports early on and Joy had a lot to say about that. She was a very competitive mother and it affected our friendship. She would say to me that my girls got into sports too soon, they were too young and I should wait until they got to high school. What happened in this friendship is that it made me question who I was. She asked my opinion then turned it around as if it never really mattered.
>
> I kept replaying the trip, how when we got on the plane and left to return, we felt defeated. Should we have stayed? I didn't know what to do as a mother and I didn't know what to do about Joy. As an adult, it was a

mess with my friend and then my daughter was suffering. Madison lost friends; she was very into sports and had friends on those teams but she was very hurt by this trip and it made me feel worse. I was in my own pain and couldn't really think clearly or help Madison.

Triangles

What could be more fraught with rivalry than a double dose of **green-eyed friends**? For Beatrice and Joy and their two fourteen-year-old daughters at the time, the strength of cliques and jealous players destroyed what they had shared as friends. As Beatrice reports the experience, the dissolution of this family friendship caused distress and anxiety. Additionally, there was a third party who contributed to the Beatrice and Madison break up with Joy and Cate:

> Because we live in the same town and both moved here at the same time, we used to get together all the time. Joy was last minute while I'm more organized. She wasn't like that. We would co-host parties for the team. I don't really know how we lasted for nine years as best friends with all the friction. We had mutual friends and that might have been part of it. One of our mutual friends said the whole thing was a nightmare, how the friendship was taken over by jealousy. When it comes to that friend, I now question her motive and think she was a schemer. She contributed to the breakup of my friendship with Joy. I believe she said a lot of things that were not true. After the trip to Las Vegas Joy and I had issues and this other friend turned on me very quickly.

Recovery

> What made me really sick, was how shaken I was, how depressed I got and I kept questioning if it was the right decision to just leave and fly back. My daughter was beside herself. Afterward, Cate and our other friend's daughter stopped talking to Madison. The girls stopped sitting with my daughter at lunch. My daughter felt very alone.
>
> A few years later Joy wanted to reconnect and said she missed our friendship. I said I was in a good place and so was Madison, I didn't want to go back because we were finally okay. I was finished and tired of giving and giving and giving with nothing in return. Besides for all the time our girls were in high school, no one from Cate's group, meaning Madison's former friends, spoke to my daughter.

While Beatrice knew Joy wanted to put it all to rest, she had agreed only for the greater good. The women lived around the corner from each other and the community had heard about it. In reality the close friendships, mother to mother/daughter to daughter were at an end:

> I will speak with Joy but in my heart we are no longer talking, I'd be going through the motions. If I run into her in the stores or the neighborhood, we are friendly, hello, how are you? I have learned I'm not the only person she had a problem with because it rests with her. I never stood up to her until that trip but the competition and jealousy started when we were class mothers for the girls in grade school, not through the kids but about the kids.
>
> What bothers me most about this whole incident and

breakup were the lies. Joy didn't believe me when I told her how I felt on that trip. I also blame myself for letting the other mother, the third friend, into our friendship. It was just more of the same thing. I look back and realize she was working to get in. She was the third wheel for sure. Now that's been over for years I know I would not do any of it again.

Madison

Cate and I had been best friends and grew up together since we were toddlers and I always thought that she and I would be just like our mothers. Our daughters would be best friends too.

•

What happened when we were all fourteen will never be completely out of my head. My best friend and I and the rest of the volleyball team were going to a tournament in Las Vegas. I was so excited because it was my mother and Cate's mother chaperoning the team and two other mothers traveling there. As soon as we left for the airport, I knew there was a problem. Before the trip began Cate was trying to make new friends in this bigger group. She and I seemed to be moving away from each other. I think we were just going in different directions because I was this sporty type and she was into being more girly. We'd both been doing sports but I had this feeling she was jealous of me and how well I was doing. It wasn't only for volleyball that I had this sense. I was more sociable and she was always with me for that. I'm the one who introduced her to my other friends.

Daughter/Daughter

Madison grew up in Douglaston, New York. Today she is in college in northern Florida, and planning to earn her master's degree:

> There was something nice about growing up with a best friend whose mother was best friends with my mother. When Joy told us we were going to travel to Las Vegas for this tournament it sounded amazing. Here was this mommy and me trip that our mothers got involved with because of their daughters. It was an opportunity to travel and spend time together. We thought we'd do sightseeing too, but when we got there and had down time we splintered into small groups that didn't work. Cate was being pushy and snarky. She made comments that were very unkind. She looked at me and said that's what you're wearing? I got so upset that I distanced myself from her. Meanwhile both our mothers were picking up on what was going on and were ready to defend their daughters. Joy was in charge and my mother was rattled, for sure the other girls all noticed what was going on. It turned into a terrible situation. Today we have no mutual friends left from being in Las Vegas.

According to Madison as well as her mother Beatrice, there was no path to redeem the trip. After three days, they decided to fly home, although it was a six-day plan. This decision was discussed with Joy, who approved, as Madison understood it. It was summer and both she and her mother thought it would blow over by the time school began in the fall. Their instincts were wrong and the event had tentacles.

Mean Girls

Afterward when I got back to school, I saw that Cate had gotten everyone to be on her side so these girls wouldn't be my friends anymore. They ganged up against me. Everyone got divided, and I felt very lonely, and my friends were on Cate's side. I look back and think maybe my mom was right and that Cate was jealous of me but the worst part was I had introduced her to these girls and that made it awful. It was the saddest time in my life. It was hard to make other friends after what my lifelong friend did to me. It was hard to trust anyone, and it took me a while to get past that. My parents put me in therapy, which wasn't their style, because they didn't know what to do with me. I didn't know how to make new friends. I'd always had these friends.

Being on other team sports helped and I was able to move on. Mostly that is because I made a new friend, someone who stood up for me and showed me what a real friend can be. She used to say to me, you are a better person, stop feeling this way. But we come from a kind of small place and news spread. All the moms knew and talked about it, all the daughters too. It seemed like Joy and Cate had done it on purpose and my mom and I were left out. But I hope it wasn't on purpose, kicking someone out—and I kept asking myself, why doesn't anyone want to be my friend? For my mom it had to be ten times worse because it wasn't just her suffering from the other mothers and what they did to her but what the daughters did to me.

Selfishness

Madison has reflected on what happened and believes it has influenced how she views female friendships. Neither she nor her mother Beatrice are involved with Joy and Cate today. She also recognizes how centered Joy was on her own children and family:

> I know it was Cate who shut me out. Those girls who listened to her will say hi to me when I'm back home from school, but I could never build the trust up. I will say hello but they would not be my friends again. I remember how Cate was about herself, how she pushed me away and could only think of pitting these girls against me.
>
> Jealousy is something I think Cate and her mom felt about my mom and me because we were so close. We have always hung out together while Cate and her mom were always in arguments. Even back then, Cate didn't talk to her mom for periods of time and I was always with my mom. I look back and she resented my closeness with my mom. All she thought of was herself and what she could do to people. Cate turned on me very much on purpose and left me in the dust. She stopped talking to me and then the other girls stopped talking to me. I knew she was wrong and selfish to do what she did. I didn't deserve it, I deserved better.

A study, *Aggression in Women: Behavior, Brain and Hormones*, by Denson, O'Dean, Blake and Beames found that females are more likely to engage in indirect forms of verbal aggression. This includes gossip or starting rumors about their peers. While we, as adult women, know what it is like to be emotionally injured by a female friend, witnessing our daughters endure the same is twice as painful. It is impressive that Madison has a high level of self-awareness and has contemplated the scenario and outcome.

Female Agency

> When I met my best friend after that year and she helped me forget the past, it still took years. I really don't think it was until my senior year in high school that I was over it.
>
> What I learned is that friendship is huge. When you have these friendships and little things like snide comments and ignoring you and rolling your eyes happen, you have to walk away. I'd never go back to those girls.
>
> I have no idea what Cate's doing with her life, but I do think she was out to ruin mine. It helped me weirdly because I saw if she won, it would be difficult and wrong. If I met her today, I wouldn't let her get away with anything. I heard she's still at home while I've branched out happily and moved to Florida for school. I'm in college, doing well. She forced me to open my eyes to experiences and I know that I will go to grad school and have a career in business, which is my goal. Everything worked out in the end because I met new people and got away.

Can This Friendship Be Saved?

A mother and daughter who both suffered in the hands of their supposed best friends is a disturbing story. Beatrice and Madison's narratives describe being ambushed and unprepared for the level of harm caused by Joy and Cate. With truly jealous friends—for females of any age—the one who is the object of these feelings is baffled and bruised. When friends are blatantly unkind, it is up to the recipients to stand up for themselves. They need to own it and either adjust their expectations or walk away.

For Beatrice and Madison there was no choice but to leave the mother/daughter friendships. Joy and Cate had diminished them and for a period they had lost faith. However they eventually extricated themselves emotionally and physically.

After the loss and sorrow that stemmed from this treatment, it is impressive that Beatrice and Madison prevailed. As it were they became the final estrangers since neither sought future contact with Joy or Cate. Their boundaries are solid and separating from what transpired has been key to their happiness and self-worth.

In these narratives we realize why jealousy is so negative and will hurt both sides. More options for women—look at Madison's achievements—lead to more female agency and a clearer view of the downside of female rivalry.

CHAPTER SEVEN

A Thieving Friend

Is she eyeing what you have?
Has she asked about your idea then stolen it?
Is she out to win at your game?
Do you think she's hiding her aspirations?
Is she after your partner, your job, your friends?

If any of these questions apply to you and your friend, there is little that is sacred in this friendship. Rather, there is great angst and a lack of transparency.

> You are very reluctant to tell your best friend (at work and in life) about your new love interest. It is this crazy feeling, as if your news will become her news, she could snatch it away from you. In fact, there is little you would tell her these days after what happened last time. Sure, it was your fault for confiding in her but she basically took your pitch for work and stole it from you. When

you tried to explain this to your boss, she raised her eyebrows suspiciously like you were the one who was taking the idea.

It's a shame too because on top of infuriating you, your friend has offended you. You ask yourself, why are you still friends? But you know the answer—several times you tried to disentangle yourself and it wasn't successful. First of all you share these friends and you and she go way back. Plus you have worked together before, at a different company. You are the one who recommended she come here, that she follow you. You even spoke with your supervisor and praised her. You have to appear supportive, keeping up an image, being cooperative colleagues and friends.

You're kicking yourself that you've been open with her, told her so many things because it hasn't served you well. She's someone who takes your ideas and claims them as her own beyond work too. For example, when you told her you wanted to go out west to rock climb and described it in detail. Suddenly she planned the exact trip with her sister. That alone isn't bothersome except it happened at a time when you and your boyfriend were hitting a rough patch. She began acting like you, using your tone and favorite phrases. When you mentioned this to him, he defended her. He said she's a good friend, a good person, what is bothering you? You let it slide and talked yourself out of your suspicions. Two weeks ago, you got a call from your aunt. She spotted this friend and your boyfriend at lunch together. They looked like a couple. It was the very day this friend had turned you down to go shoe shopping at noon. Isn't the writing on the wall?

Delusions

When a friend takes what is precious to you, be it your sister or lover or genius idea, it falls into the category of a thieving friend. In the previous chapter, we read of friends who are rivalrous, wanting to win and not having their closest friends' best interests at heart. In this chapter it is taken a step further, your friend is not simply jealous, but will take what is yours. We are now in the thieving zone. Let's consider Oprah Winfrey's take on this in her interview with Melinda French Gates when she stated, "You can't really be friends with anybody who has a hint of jealousy about anything that you're doing."

In Kate Murphy's opinion piece in the *New York Times*, "Do Your Friends Actually Like You?" she writes about the friends we assume feel the same toward us as we do toward them. Yet they do not return the level of feeling and are not good for our health. An MIT Media Lab study, "Friendship Reciprocity and Behavioral Change," found only fifty percent of the time are friendships reciprocal and only half of these friendships are truly mutual.

These findings reverberate in what proves to be a never-ending game of the 'glittering prizes.' Depending upon what we are taught to strive for and one's personal desires, the checklist includes professional success, men, beauty, children, career, and lifestyle. With the thieving friend the stakes are raised. There is the possibility of losing what we've achieved and it proves exhausting. A high level of estrangement kicks in and whatever intimacy was shared between the two friends can be shattered.

Despite the great gains that women have made in the twenty-first century—earning power and career, education, choices in partnering or not—women of every age are aware of the 'reach.' We are encouraged to measure ourselves only against other women, including our friends. This stirs up constant dissatisfaction. Add to that the friends we encounter who want what we have and it ratchets up to the next level. Often times we instinctively feel they will try to take what we have. For example, as mentioned earlier, in *Desperate Housewives*, women were pitted against each other. The single women on the street, played by Teri Hatcher and Nicollette Sheridan, vied for Mike (James Denton), the plumber. Not only because he was available and attractive, but because whoever nabbed him would win. The classic film, *Working Girl*, starring Melanie Griffith and Sigourney Weaver, is about two women wanting the same man and job, which Griffith's character snaps up. We are reminded that we live in a world of limited goods—no wonder there are thieving friends. Consider the following scenarios:

Robyn, 45, lives in Dallas, Texas and is a publicist. She has twin sons and is a single mother:

> It takes a while for me to feel I have a close friend, so I was watching. I saw how this friend operated. I saw she had a need to eclipse me. Still, she was a fun friend. Sort of an equal in our dating search. But our ending proves she did not consider me a close friend. We were friends for ten years. She knew my boyfriend and he told her he didn't think I cared enough for him. So she asked me if I was serious with him. I think she was upset that I had connected to someone. Beyond that, maybe she was sorry she and he were not together. She was competitive so she didn't like that I was with this guy. That I had gotten the guy and she had not found someone. I had this sinking feeling when this happened, like I'd be on the outs with her. We were in our forties, we weren't in high school or college but it felt like we were. We had

the same goals, to find someone who would be open to our children and had been around themselves. But the issues were the same issues as before—who gets the guy and who wins. Jealousy was a part of it, she was very jealous. She knew this man. I think they had dated a while back. So she decided once he was with me, she wanted him back. It was too much, way more than plain jealousy. I had to escape.

Like Robyn, Jean bonded with a friend over their singlehood only to learn that the cost to the friendship was too great. Jean, 68, lives in Cleveland and works in the arts. She is divorced with four grown children and four grandchildren:

Eleven years ago, I met this one woman through mutual friends. We were both single and that sort of bound us together. I reached out to her about being in a city and dating at an older age. She fashioned herself as taking me under her guidance and taught me things. She was looking for a wing man and had it figured out. She could have three men ordering drinks for her, that's how she worked. I was attractive enough to be her sidekick. It was my role. She knew where to find the men and together we shopped for sexy lingerie. There was no depth or sincerity in her quest for me to be her close friend. Her goal was for us to work together to find the men. She came from a different world: she was widowed and she and her husband had been in love. She had lost that life and could never recapture it. I was divorced, it wasn't the same, only that we were both out there as single women at a certain age. We had that to share. She was very scrappy and hardboiled. I didn't realize her agenda at first and we spent a lot of time together. When I met someone, she thought he was hers. She wasn't going to watch me have this success. That ended the friendship and since we didn't go way back, it was okay for me to leave. I didn't have guilt or regret, I just had her number.

Sarrie, 29, moved to Iowa City a year ago, where she works at a hair salon. She was married three months ago and has no children:

> Since I am in a new place to live and to work, the one friend I made means something. She and I do everything together. We both work at the salon and when I first got there, she was welcoming. But she noticed I'm good at what I do and some of her clients are now asking for me. This really upset her and she has made comments. She's about my age and also married, so the friendship is not only about us but we're friends as couples. Last week the biggest client at the salon wanted me to color and blow out her hair. This friend lost it. Now she is trying hard to not only get her back but take my clients that were never hers to begin with. She's gone to the owner to complain and we're supposed to be friends. I don't want to be her friend anymore but I'm here. We're at the same job and our husbands play pickleball together.

Expiration Dates

The mixture of closeness with jealousy that turns into thieving is a sharp contrast to strong female friendships. Lillian Schlissel's book, *Women's Diaries of the Westward Journey* documents the lives and feelings of women who travelled west in the mid-nineteenth century. They wrote home to those friends they'd left behind, expressing how painful it was to be separated from them. These women were totally positive about their feelings while the twenty-first century friendships noted in this chapter are bifurcated. This is not to say that thieving didn't exist among women centuries ago—we've read about it in Edith Wharton and Jane Austen novels. On the other hand, sophisticated, modern life with its many facets can fuel the many ways in which thieving occurs in negative friendships.

"The Friendship Challenge," Mary Gaitskill's *New Yorker* essay, describes her own friendship decades ago and the part that envy and theft played in it. "The envy I felt for her *was* about who we were, as well as about our perceived value as girls," she writes. A thieving friend can be jealous or envious but rather than wanting her friend to fail, she covets what her friend has. That means taking is winning while also an embodiment of the friend whom she cares about. In an occasional twist the predictable estranger who would be the one who has been robbed, is not estranging. Instead, she might be the estrangee while the one who is robbing is the one who cuts off the friendship.

For instance, Katherine, 44, a graphic designer who lives in Milwaukee, is shocked by what occurred with her best friend:

> My husband and I were at a concert with our close friends—the wife was my best friend and maid of honor at our wedding. We were describing the house we wanted to buy and had bid on. It was in a very popular area for couples with small children. We were very excited and hopeful and told these friends in confidence. The next day we heard that we were outbid and someone else had snapped it up. It was this couple who had done it. They listened to us describe it then bought it from under us. My instinct was to never speak to her again,

except our boys are friends and we are part of the same community. What happened next was surprising—my best friend stopped talking to me. She started ignoring my texts and calls including ones about the kids getting together. When they moved into the house, they had a big party and we were not invited. Sometimes I wish we could move out of town, all of this has been too disturbing.

Penelope, 51, living in northern California where she works in the construction business, recalls the end of an important friendship:

In 2016 this friendship ended. We'd known each other since college in the nineties, but I wasn't totally surprised when she 'iced' me. Still, I'm not sure what I did that offended her. I know what she did, she stopped having time and energy for me and began to be with our mutual friend. This came between us but it was her fault and then she left me.

We lived two towns over in the Bay area. We shared other friends and did things together. She stopped responding to my texts and phone calls. When we finally spoke, that was it. There was no confrontation. I had no idea why she found fault with me. She just cut me off. We had been so close and now I've lost two friends because she has turned against me and has told our mutual friend to do the same. The other friend she took from me—it's all wrong and beyond me.

Larina, 56, living in Vermont, is perplexed by how her relationship with a thieving friend transpired. She is married with two daughters and works as a librarian:

My friend and I never really reconciled after this one encounter. We fought over money. She left a restaurant and avoided paying her part of the meal. She left us with the bill. We had been friends for years and years and I had to chase down the money. If you can believe it, she blamed me. She decided it was my fault after it was really a free meal. It wasn't the money, of course, it was what it meant.

That's left us without a real friendship. We will see each other and be cordial, there is small talk. But it's awkward. I saw her at a luncheon and she wouldn't discuss it. I'm not sure what she thinks. She is angry over such a stupid thing. Didn't she steal a meal? One day I hope to get in the presence of this friend and we can talk about it. But what happened has never been fixed. She doesn't want to see me and so we've lost touch. She was the closest person to me in my life. I'd love to know what I did when I know what she did. It's a mess because we were so friendly.

Paradox

Relationships with a thieving friend are complex. An opportunistic friend may, on the one hand, want what the other friend has. But she can also be caring and emotionally supportive in other ways. The connection between the friends runs deep and the notion of severing it can be too stressful to contemplate.

In an abstract by MacDonald and Leary, "Why Does Social Exclusion Hurt? The relationship between social and physical pain," the authors put forth the idea that being excluded affects us in a biological way. This reaction is evolutionary and as we have seen in these pages, is understandable. Being blown off by a friend can cause physical pain as well as being an emotional loss.

A famous friendship that caused great distress is that of Mary Todd Lincoln and Elizabeth Keckley. Elizabeth Keckley was Mary Todd Lincoln's dressmaker and confidante. The bond between the two women began with such promise and ended with bad faith. When Mrs. Keckley published her book in 1868, *Behind the Scenes,* about her slavery and her years with the Lincolns in the White House, pages about the first family were interpreted as crossing the line. The Virginia Museum of History and Culture reports that the friendship ended at this point.

Double Dealing

A very different kind of breach is in the film *Single White Female,* starring Bridget Fonda (Allie) and Jennifer Jason Leigh (Hedy). We witness the dark side of female bonding when two young women become roommates. The friendship starts quickly but it is Hedy's increasing anger and jealousy that drives the story. She eerily wants the same clothes and haircut as Allie, as if she's taking over her life. She also manipulates the rapport that Allie has with her boyfriend, discouraging her from the relationship.

As Allie watches Hedy carry off parts of her very soul, she realizes she has to do something. While few of us may have experienced such a dire outcome to a friendship, this is a cautionary tale.

In real life several interviewees reported the far-reaching consequences of a friend who filches one's boyfriend or partner. For example, Clarice, 22, living in Philadelphia where she works in a family business, has been betrayed in this manner by her thieving friend:

> My bf is no longer my bf. She slept with my ex-boyfriend. He and I were together for three years and she and I were childhood best friends. She had a boyfriend at the time and then they broke up. She came and confessed as if our friendship wasn't important at all. I told her she should confess to her boyfriend too. After that I cut ties with both my ex and with this friend. I heard through friends that she and my ex-boyfriend went away together. They were a couple for a long time before I figured it out I think, behind my back. I didn't see it coming.
>
> I can't trust anyone anymore because my bf decided to choose a man over me. I can't be with any women friends today. I'm too hurt. I just started dating someone new and we'll see. I have new female friends now but I have a lot of fears after what my best friend did to me. It isn't the same. I won't be as close to these other women because it could happen again.

Jodi, 52, living on the west coast of Florida where she is a headhunter, is shaken by how destructive her trusted friend has proven to be. Jody has a grown child and is single:

> When I got divorced eleven years ago, my best friend from a baby and me class when our kids were small, went after my ex-husband. I was very surprised because she had supported me throughout the divorce, taking my side, really. We had been friends with our kids. So I confronted her and she said it just happened, it wasn't planned. I guess she always wanted him, that's why she badmouthed him when I did, in hopes my marriage would totally be over. That's why I doubted her defense. I look back on it and see that she encouraged me to be divorced

so that could happen. She needed me to set him free for her so it could look innocent. She has done something very ugly. Now I'm single and without this best friend.

Sister Escape

For our sister story in this chapter, I've chosen Cassandra, 37, who lives in Maine, where she feels "far enough away" from her sister, Dia, 29, who lives in southern Connecticut. For years Cassandra felt her place as eldest in the family created her the pleaser daughter and 'big sister.'

> My younger sister, who I tried to be close to and to protect, was always difficult. When she was a teenager, I lied for her plenty to our parents. I asked her to be careful what she did with her friends. I know I was perceived as the goody two shoes older sister. But she was the youngest and I'd already helped my twin brothers get through their adolescence. What I learned about this sister that always bothered me, from the time she was in sixth grade, was how she would take anything from a friend. She was competitive and sort of sneaky.
>
> As the years went on and we were both adults, it got worse. I went to medical school while my little sister didn't even finish college. She couldn't take my achievement from me but she acted like it was nothing. When I moved to a nice house, she said to me, I'm sorry, why is that your house, how did you land that husband? To me, relocating with my family was the only way to escape. The distance helps and has made it much easier than if I'd have to act on separating. I'm too far for us to

make plans. This is after years of wondering if I had the guts to leave my sister. What is complicated is the relief I feel to not be with my sister.

Hence this chapter brings us to the steps we take when our suboptimal friendships and sister narratives weigh too heavily. Amy Banks, author of *Wired to Connect: The Surprising Link Between Brain Science and Strong, Healthy Relationships*, writes about the pluses of gratifying connections. She notes these links are what we need to strengthen neural pathways in our brains that encourage closeness and connection. For those of us who experience the opposite, Banks' research sheds light on negative situations. We realize in certain instances, estrangement is a useful, successful alternative.

The soul searching in this chapter yields answers.

How worn out are you from this friendship?

When your friend is blatantly after what is yours—often something you've worked diligently to achieve—it is exhausting. This is a warning that you need to end the chaos of it all.

Have you noticed that lessening the time you spend together isn't enough?

It would be best if you finished the pretense that things are okay with this friend. If you own that you are unhappy, it gives you agency.

Do you imagine what a better life it would be if this friend wasn't going after what is yours?

With a thieving friend, compromises are not easy. It's an all or nothing proposition. If you face who she is, you will be better equipped to be the **estranger** and leave her behind.

Despite all that you know about this friend, why are you conflicted about letting go?

For so many of us there is still the allure of the friend and a sentimental view of the friendship. If she is out to have what is yours, it is time to rethink your part of it.

Do you wonder about her perception of her actions?

Some thieving friends have a lot to bring to the friendship, that's the irony. From their perspective, the friendship is successful. Others who want what belongs to their friends are very conscious of their actions.

Can you let go and feel vindicated?

In the brave new world of estrangement, women of all ages are able to extricate themselves with a strong sense of self. Often they regret it didn't work out and their feelings for the friend are many-sided, but estrangement is key.

SHE SAID / SHE SAID
EXHIBIT G: Dicey Triangles

Taylor and Sally

In this chapter we'll look at Sally and Taylor, both 49, who had a longstanding, solid friendship until Taylor started dating Sally's brother. The entire friendship was put at risk and whatever intimacy was shared between the two friends was shattered.

Sally

> I begged Taylor not to be with my brother, I knew he was destructive. She said I was manipulative and jealous.
>
> •
>
> Years ago my best friend Taylor started running around with my brother and I was left behind with our other friends, which was awkward without her. Plus everyone knew they couldn't last, that he was poison, but what happened to our friendship because they were a couple was so painful. She and I began to dissolve, as if we'd never been best friends and we had been for decades.
>
> I was the middle child and had a happy childhood. My younger sister and older brother and I are close today. I came from a family-oriented family. It never occurred to me that my brother, years after Taylor and I had been best friends, would start dating her. It became this huge drama and I was caught in the middle.

While we have witnessed a lack of boundaries among friends and sisters, when siblings mix with friends it can prove an intricate web. To make matters worse in the triangle of Sally, Bill and Taylor, there was a second triangulated relationship threatening the Sally/Taylor twosome. Sally and Taylor shared a third friend, Audrey, who was a part of their best friendship in high school. As we will see, this trio had its ups and downs.

Triplex

Today Sally, a grade schoolteacher, living in Newport, Rhode Island, is proud of raising her daughters alone. She reflects on her friendship with Taylor and feels it has taught her a great deal about herself. Her rich history with this friend is why she was so disturbed by the estrangement that took place:

> Taylor and I did not go to the same school and it was Audrey who knew us both and made the introduction. The three of us hung out all the time. From when we were fifteen, we were known as a threesome. We did everything together. When it came to college, Taylor and I were right next door to each other in the same college town. We saw each other on weekends and Audrey was out of state. Taylor and I were closer during those days. We did sports and then the social stuff. We went to movies, parties, to the mall, and travelled together. We rented a house in the Hamptons together for a lot of summers, starting when we were in college. We'd go there as a group and we did girl weekends in Miami. Taylor and I were besties wherever we went, whatever we did.

After earning her associate degree and then her bachelor degree in education, Sally became engaged. She broke this off, deciding her fiancé was 'bossy':

> I was relieved to cancel the wedding. Later I felt pressure to be married and raise a family. During this time, Audrey had moved to the Midwest. She'd gotten married when we were very young. So she missed this part, where Taylor was and I were living nearby. At some point Taylor was married then divorced. We were in touch all the time.

Enmeshed

Soon after Taylor's divorce she and Sally's brother Bill began to date. Their families knew each other, and Bill had always been merely Sally's big brother. This conveyed an implicit, acceptable space that was evaporating once their romance began.

> First Bill and Taylor were together and it was shocking. I warned her. He was drinking too much and he womanized. I was close with Bill but I didn't think he should date Taylor. I told them both and neither of them listened. I kept saying it was a bad idea. They'd get into these terrible fights. Then I would explain to my brother why Taylor did what she did. I'd say that she had been in such a bad marriage so she was acting out. Then he'd go back and tell her what I said, probably twisting what I meant. I asked Bill to stop telling Taylor but he didn't. Their relationship was never solid. She was coming off a terrible relationship and so was he. I saw all the crazy

stuff that they did to each other, and I said, you should not date. I told Taylor, Bill is your best friend's brother, that's all. Once they were dating, it became a family situation.

While they were a couple I weened myself away from them. I wasn't okay with them being together, but I didn't know how to be heard. My sister was hoping they wouldn't date too and once they began, that it would stop soon. She was worried that something bad would happen. We knew our brother. He had been a womanizer always and now he was also hurt by what happened with his ex-wife. He is an artistic type, not athletic at all. He could be reactive. He is a chef and temperamental. Both Taylor and I are athletic, Taylor more than I am.

My sister and parents and I begged and pleaded with my brother to stop seeing Taylor. He was always over at her house and it was very uncomfortable for me, I was used to being at her house but not then. Meanwhile, I was dating someone I really cared about and I was happy. Then Bill and Taylor began to fight. These were bad fights, but I'd warned her, do not go with him. She and I tried to stay best friends during the whole ordeal. But it wasn't really okay. There was Bill's side and there was Taylor's side. Everything blew up. I was very upset. I would have rather lost touch with my brother than with Taylor. She didn't know that but it is how I felt. I could have said it in a fight with her during this whole ordeal and not remember, but I honestly believe she never knew how much she meant to me. We were splitting up over my brother. I couldn't believe it.

Broken

For Sally, the pain seemed to fan out and the estrangements were in every direction. As she describes it, she was no longer grounded:

> While this was happening with Bill and Taylor and my boyfriend, Audrey was back. As a friend she was such fun, I liked her a lot when we were young. I thought she was a great friend. But as we got older, I saw that she was only into herself. Her husband walked out on her and she had been so far from home with two very small children. Taylor and I did everything for her and she did nothing for us, no effort.
>
> It got much worse with Audrey for me when Taylor and Bill broke up. Audrey was the one with kids. We were still single. Audrey would listen to Taylor's side of the story when it came to Bill—all about my brother and the things he said. She would sympathize with Taylor. Then there was the fighting with Audrey. We were all thirty years old and no one got along.
>
> At the same time the relationship with the man I liked so much didn't end up working out and it was awful. It was right after Taylor and I stopped talking. She wasn't there to know my pain. I thought she would have liked him. I had lost Taylor and then I lost the boyfriend.
>
> In the following months—for the next year or more, I was sad and didn't see things clearly. I dated the wrong guys. Everyone local was talking about what had happened with Taylor and Bill. My parents said very little but they were very displeased. Everyone felt bad for me. I felt such loss, I went from all these friends to empty.

It forced me to start with new friends. I dated the man who became my husband, now my ex-husband.

It wasn't that I felt betrayed as much as I felt it was all wrong. I had told both Taylor and Bill not to do it. I'd begged them. We were young, not really understanding the danger.

Failed Efforts

Two years later, I married my husband. I so missed having Taylor in my life—she was not at the wedding, we were not in touch. There would have been no wedding had she been around. I know she would have warned me not to marry the man I did. She would have talked me out of it. He was a local fireman, he was a certain type. But by this period in my life, everyone I knew was married and having kids. So I married him to fill the void. Soon after I realized it was a mistake. The minute he was my husband he changed like a chameleon. I had friends to talk to but not like I'd talk to Taylor. One of my friends was too far away, living down south, for me to be with her. I had no support. My family was not excited when I married him but they were relieved I was married. My husband was mentally abusive and horrible to me when I was pregnant. Throughout all this, I thought of Taylor. What could I do, at that point she and Audrey had moved on.

I didn't miss Audrey's friendship. I missed Taylor, more and more. I figured she thought I hadn't wished her well and it wasn't so. Once I ran into her when I was pregnant, we walked by each other. My brother moved and he didn't have to deal with the backlash. For a long while

I was angry. He never said he was sorry. He traveled for work and to this day only shows up for holidays. We still talked. We were sister and brother. There was some kind of friction between us that had remained. It was over how he handled the whole thing. Later he ended up with someone he had known through his work. My parents just shook their heads. They had been very troubled by all of it.

Ten Years Apart

When Taylor broke up with Bill, she moved away, became the estranger and stopped speaking to Sally, the estrangee. This stance lasted for ten years until Taylor returned home again. For Sally it was an uneasy situation and she dreaded running into her. At the same time, she knew it was inevitable and was conflicted:

> I'm not sure how it would have been with Taylor except our girls started playing softball and ended up on the same team. We met on the field and were polite to one another. We said things like, "good game" and "how are you?" At the game we sat near each other, we began to talk. The next year our girls were on the same team again. There was a group of mothers who became friends and we were both invited into the group. I was nervous it could blow up again or that she still hated me and my family but happy to be back in touch.
>
> Today I'll go to Taylor's house but there is no mixing with my family. We have never discussed my brother and what happened. Probably we should have had a

few conversations about it, yet we never have revisited the past. Once she said to me that she wished it never happened. I feel exactly the same. I have stayed away from the Audrey part. I want nothing to do with her and I've kept it that way. Once recently, we talked about Audrey and I said to Taylor, "I told you so."

I learned to never mix family with friends. Taylor and I are not as close now, too many awful things happened. I wish we'd never stopped speaking. It affected how I became with other friends, cautious about not rocking the boat. I have a different approach and trust is an issue for me. I am grateful that Taylor and I are back in each other's lives.

Taylor

Sally was always more outgoing while I was more reserved. She would put herself out there and was extremely social, always smiling and happy. She made it easier for me.

•

I met Sally when we were in tenth grade through Audrey. The three of us were very close and saw each other all the time. Sally and I became best friends when we were in college and we got together every weekend. We were connected in a lot of ways. Years later, there would be a drama and Audrey could not be trusted. She took both sides. Although we had a major parting, it was Sally I always counted on.

… CHAPTER SEVEN | 184 …

Estrangements

Taylor lives in Newport, RI, where she works in a family business and has been married for seventeen years. She has four children. Coming from a close-knit family, her maternal grandparents were like second parents to her. Her mother was very even in how she treated both Taylor and her brother. What influenced her greatly was that her mother and aunt stopped speaking for the last thirty years of their lives:

> When I was about sixteen I noticed my mother was separated from her sister. Suddenly we weren't talking to my aunt or my cousin anymore. When my grandma became sick, my aunt came to visit her in the hospital. Then my grandma died. My aunt came to the wake and the funeral without speaking to any of us. Soon after that my mother died, very suddenly, without ever speaking to my aunt again. For all those years I was very sad about losing touch with my cousin, my aunt's daughter. It was like my mother's side of this once close family had disintegrated. This affected me in terms of my closest friends, like Sally and Audrey. I counted on them.

To add to Taylor's family situation, Audrey had moved out of town and was going through a difficult time.

> Sally and I were a team when Audrey had big problems. Audrey had married and moved to the Midwest. He left her when their kids were little and took everything. Sally and I flew out to help her. We gave her money and helped her move back to Newport. Sally and I convinced her to get help from her family. Then things got worse, still we

were there. In the middle of Audrey's troubles, she and Sally had a falling out. I stayed in touch with her but she was not talking to Sally. Our threesome had been broken but I was friends with both. Sally and I were still very close. But I felt like with my family and friends it was a bad place.

Roller Coaster

After the turmoil and separation that Taylor describes, it's understandable that she wanted her two best friends to be stand-ins for family, from whom she was estranged:

> I got married for the first time when I was very young. Sally was at the wedding, so was Audrey. The marriage was an awful experience and didn't last long. It was a quick window of about two years, a time when you really lean on your friends. Sally was there for me.
>
> Not long after my divorce I was at a party with Sally and Sally's older brother, Bill, came. He was also just divorced and we started dating. Sally seemed okay with it but it's very difficult with your best friend's brother. If she was unhappy, she accepted it. She was willing to try to make it work and I saw that about her. It got tense when I wasn't available to do things with Sally because I was with Bill. When Bill began drinking too much, he and I argued. Soon after the crap began with Bill and he pulled Sally into our relationship. When it got rockier Bill decided to spill his two sisters' true feelings about me. I was devastated. Now I look back and I'm not sure how much of what their brother said was true. Sally and I had

a confrontation. She apologized. But I was stubborn and I wasn't going to give in. It became too much. At first we were in a feud and then the time went on and on and we were not friends anymore.

For ten years Taylor and Sally were not on speaking terms. During this time, Taylor remarried and was raising a family.

Sally didn't come to my second wedding and I didn't go to hers although I heard she was getting married again. It was terrible when we were broken up, like having a severed limb. We had been there for every milestone, for everything in our lives and then she was gone.
To make matters worse Audrey was pleased that Sally and I weren't talking, she was thrilled. She loved when we weren't in touch. Even in the middle of her tragedies including a death in her family, she liked any kind of gossip and disruption. After her husband left her and her sibling died, she never wanted anyone else to be happy again. She wanted to poison the water with her misery. For her the best part was that I might talk about Sally. Years earlier she had tried to wedge us apart, playing multiple hands. I see now that Audrey had a problem with the truth, she told more and more lies. First she'd lied to Sally and then to me. So I stepped away from Audrey too. I don't think she wanted to be a part of my life and made excuses to not see me, She was single at that point while I was home with my babies. It had gotten complicated and it was Sally who was my confidante, the only one I trusted to share my secrets. She knew who I really was. When Audrey fell out, I was probably relieved. It was Sally I missed—I could let Audrey go.

Do-Over

In this narrative, Audrey became a thieving friend as she tried and succeeded in stealing Taylor from Sally. Already there was the Sally, Taylor, Bill triangle that caused repercussions with the family. This damage took years to heal. However, it's worth remembering that before the Taylor dated Bill, Sally and Taylor had a deep commitment to each other and an authentic friendship:

> It wasn't until I had my children that I realized how important my friendship with Sally had been. I didn't have a sister so she was 'my sister.' I don't recall who reached out first or triggered our conversation. I was thinking was how silly this had been and we needed to talk about our breakup. The longer we didn't speak, the easier it was for the person to be out of your life. Time goes so fast. I've struggled with what happened. We had vowed as kids to always be there for one another. I feel I wasn't there for the breakdown of her marriage when she needed me.

Recently, Sally and Taylor have reconnected. Taylor feels that the years alone have taught her what to value in a friendship.

> Sally and I went through so much because of Bill. It was easier at the time to act like I was fifteen and run away from it. I didn't give back to her as she did for me.
> I should not have gone with him. I know that now.
> He and I never spoke again and I heard he moved out of town. I look back and realize who mattered. Today Sally and I are together again and we try our best. We do not talk about her brother. If Sally needed anything, I would be there in a heartbeat. I have learned how to be a better

friend by having lost Sally all those years. We have apologized to one another. I know now, I would have taken Sally over Bill any day.

Our relationship is not as close as it was, we have been busy with our kids—I have four and she has two. We have been careful. But we were able to rebuild our friendship and I know I only have to make a phone call and Sally would be there.

Can This Friendship Be Saved?

Unlike the Helen/Gabriella narrative in Exhibit C where despite a deep commitment that once existed, the two friends are not reconciled, Taylor and Sally are in touch after ten years apart. Their children, who were quite small when the two friends were estranged, are included. The Taylor/Sally/Bill situation and the Taylor/Sally/Audrey situation are dispelled. What prevails is the friendship of Sally and Taylor.

As Gwendolyn Poppe writes in her essay "The Harsh Reality of Losing Your Best Friend to Their Boyfriend," once a romance begins, the single friend can be 'cast away' and eventually 'phased out.' In these predicaments comprised of two best female friends and a romantic partner who comes on the scene, if one of the players feels neglected, it becomes problematic. The Sally/Taylor/Bill trigon is more loaded because it involves Sally's brother. When Kendall Jenner dated Anwar Hadid, her best friends' Bella and Gigi's brother, an article, "Should You Date Your BFF's Sibling?" ran in *DNA*. Psychologist Seema Hingorrany is quoted, saying. "If you have fallen for your BFF's sibling, it's best to let them know first, to avoid any misunderstandings in the future." If not approached this way, there can be a rift.

The full disclosure and level of honesty in both Sally and Taylor's stories indicates how important the friendship was and remains to both women. They are very aware of the repercussions of being reunited and regretful that their problem became as dire as it did.

When it came to the Audrey piece, they realized, independent of each other, how it wasn't a helpful connection. A decade long silence between two best friends is a long period of time and we respect their reconciliation.

PART THREE

How We Defriend

CHAPTER EIGHT

The Breakup/Ghosting

Have there been too many incidents?

Are you out of tricks to preserve this friendship?

Have you hit your threshold?

Do you imagine life would be better without her?

Is what she has done unforgivable?

If your answer is yes to any of the above questions, it is time to move on.

> Your best friend caused psychic pain and unrest for ages. What began on a high note is gone and any happy times are a memory. When you first became so close, she was a sounding board for your concerns and you trusted her. She totally had your back. In return you offered her the same level of support and loyalty. Besides, you have a shared history, you met the men you married when you were roommates, and you cheered each other on as you

built your careers. When you had a baby first, you asked her to be godmother. When she had her first child, you guided her in terms of preschools and day care. For years this friendship was one you could both rely on.

Once your friend's husband left her and she lost her job, things shifted. She had two sons to get through high school and had to sell the house and move to a smaller one. You were there for her throughout, including hosting her boys for a ski trip on winter break. Since her husband abandoned his sons, your husband took them to sports events and tried to fill in. But your friend's bitterness overwhelmed any of your efforts and mostly she was very angry at everyone, including you. She lashed out when your older son was the wrestling champ, saying she was surprised and wondered if he was actually deserving.

She compared her divorce to your sister's divorce and said nasty things about your sister's ex-husband's fathering that were not true. You are not only surprised but on the defensive. Each time you make a plan, she complains your life is a bed of roses. She recently remarked that it was the luck of the draw that you're still married to your husband. She asked if you are convinced he is faithful.

At the book club you both joined seven years ago, she said if the next novel is your selection your taste was too soppy and commercial. This was surprising since you and she have the same taste in books. Despite her attitude, you asked your cousin to invite her to a cocktail party where a nice widower was invited too. When you got there, this man had the flu and had cancelled. Your friend was irate. She began screaming at you that it was never really going to happen. That everything you do is questionable, that you are a selfish, too fortunate person.

Then she stormed out. That night when you got home, you deleted her from your social media and blocked her from your contact list. You told your sons they could be friendly with her sons, but could not invite them to your house. In the ensuing months, this friend has reached out to you numerous times, including sending a letter of apology via fed ex. You have not replied. Finally she has stopped her attempts. You do not want to ever go back to what was.

Spiraling

A friend who pushes us to the edge, as in the composite, reminds us that life events often influence a friendship. Of course what drives a friendship to estrangement is also about the character of the friends—and difficult conditions provoke what seems like a shocking change in character. In the amalgam above, the friend might or might not have become hostile and contrary if her marriage and her position at work had remained in place. But once her life was altered, she most clearly resented her best friend's stable existence. That is when a surprising aspect of her personality became apparent.

Karen Horney, founder of The American Institute for Psychoanalysis, believed that each of us has a need for emotional safety. Her view was that our culture has a role in spinning us toward our authentic selves, healthy friendships and unavoidable splits. When we contemplate this, we know that without respect and honesty among friends, breakups are unavoidable. Over sixty percent of the women in this study said a close female friend had severed ties with them. When there is an actual blow-up, it has a profound effect on an intimate friendship. This stirs a sense of rising agitation, a questioning of the friend's moral code. An emotional withdrawal follows—there is a coldness in the relationship that was never present before. At first your contact becomes limited, obligatory, an uneasy alliance. What follows is often a physical disconnect where you do not spend time with the friend. At that point in the friendship, a breakup seems inevitable.

Consider Mara, 34, who works in data analytics and is single, living in Seattle:

> I have been friendly with one woman for the past nine years and we've shared every experience, every secret possible. We are so close I haven't even needed a steady boyfriend. Except now this friend decided to take a job on the east coast without telling me. I found out on Instagram. It makes me wonder how I ever trusted her. Or if it's worth staying in touch, I mean what for?

For Quiet, 37, married and in the food industry in Detroit, a friendship also seems finite. She has made her decision based on what has occurred with her best friend. As with several previous narratives where a friend sleeps with her best friend's partner or boyfriend, estrangement is the result:

> Growing up I only had two best friends and one died. The other slept with my boyfriend. This happened eight years ago. I walked into my house, he and I lived together. She was in bed with my boyfriend. She had a boyfriend at the time too. She begged us to stay together and apologized, She said men come and go and tried to make light of it.
> I broke up with that boyfriend and left the friend. I think it was going on with the two of them for a long time. Before that I thought we had a real friendship. There was a level of trust as bf's that was over. There was no point.

> She was out of my life. I couldn't miss someone who does that to you.

While Mara and Quiet are entering estrangement as the estranger, Ray, 61, a social worker living in Tennessee, laments being the estrangee in a lifetime friendship:

> My best friend and I grew up the same hometown and have had the same group of friends for fifty years. Recently one of our mutual friends had a dinner party—women only—and she wasn't invited. She asked me to intervene and insist she be included. I had no sway and this friend thinks I sold her out. I keep calling her and texting. She won't listen to my side. After a lifetime of being so close she's decided we can't be together.

Repeat Blow Ups

Although we know that not all friendships have a knock down drag out ending, outbursts between friends can lead to estrangements. Repeat patterns of fighting and then a slow return to the friendship mirrors a known issue in romantic relationships and marriages. In *Coming Back from and Breaking the Cycle of Toxic Fighting in Your Relationship*, clinician Xavier Heditsian of the Naya Clinic views this as a cycle of avoidance and denial of feelings that "only keeps partners feeling more disconnected and distant."

For friendships that have gone through blowups along with hurtful scenes, the remedy of expressing emotions and rebuilding isn't on the table. Consider Nadine, 46, a medical technician living in the Berkshires. What transpired with her best friend was a 'deal breaker.'

I thought my friends were dropping me because I'd gotten to a certain place. When I moved in with my fiancé ten years ago I was 36 and overripe. My best friend at the same office where I worked, who was single, was offended that I'd 'crossed over.' I thought she was dumping me but I was the one, I gave up our friendship to start a life that led to marriage. She and I had shared so much and for a decade we had taken care of each other. Then she was abandoned by me. What makes it worse is that she became abusive. She would yell at me about this man in public places. We were at a party and she was speaking too loud, saying she was supposed to be married first. I had to move past her for lots of reasons. But really it was the fighting that ruined our friendship. We have not spoken since. I guess I should be sad but I'm relieved.

Closet Cleaning

Despite how intense and affecting best female friendships can be, as we know, there is no guidebook for how to handle a breakup. We understand divorce among married couples. There is a template and it is a known quantity. We are informed of celebrity divorces; it is a common theme in literature, film and streaming. Marriage, as it is defined for us, is meant to last, even though we readily understand news of someone's divorce. As Margaret Mead, the social anthropologist, famously said, "We have got to face that marriage is a terminable institution."

In listening to the interviewees and the depths of despair in situations with their female friends, I realized that female friendships as well, are "terminable," even though they're not technically "institutions." Because our female friendships are integral and intimate, when they implode, the breakups, as complicated as they may be, free us. As does leaving a disintegrating marriage.

A novel that shows us the root of our female bonds is *Swing Time* by Zadie Smith. Her book follows two young women, both dancers, who are jealous enough that it undermines the friendship. Celebrity female friendships where there has been a fracture include Winona Ryder and Gwyneth Paltrow's upset over who landed the *Shakespeare in Love* role, as reported in *MamaMia.com* and Jennie Garth and Tiffani Thiessen who worked on *Beverly Hills 90210* together, as reported in *Us Weekly*. In everyday life, we see it, know, it, live it—as women in this book attest to.

Shelley, 48, working in the tech industry, living in a northern city, tells us about the time after her breakup with an important friend:

> You can end up being the victim, even if you trust the friend. I felt victimized by her actions after it was over. I'm still able to have close friendships but it isn't easy. When a relationship ends, it ends. I don't go about methodically making things up, this one was on her. She had a position of power and she would push things around. She would invite me then disinvite me, lie about her plans, talk about how important her other friends were while I felt like I didn't matter. I felt confused and all her mean acts made me question myself. Today I have nice female friends and I've learned what to look for. One friend who is twelve years younger and I share a healthy friendship, There's never a harsh word. I learned how to do that by leaving the friend who hurt me, someone

who abused power. I would not have become close to her if I had seen how hostile a person she was. It was a lightning rod. I provoked her too. I'm not innocent. I hold a grudge but I also was able to let go.

Dora, 60, a freelancer who writes about travel, has no children. She is relieved to have left a close friend behind. Married twice, she is presently single:

> I was not regretful that we broke up because it was like she wanted to be friends to mistreat me. She was competitive and she would insult me, say I looked awful when it wasn't true. She talked about everyone so I knew I was part of her conversation when we weren't together. She made fun of women who were involved with their children and grandchildren. Like they didn't know what they were doing.
>
> I saw her dark side, how she could be. It takes two I kept saying, making excuses. This was an isolated situation, I told myself. I hung in for too long. They say over 60 it's hard to make new female friends but I'm lucky, I've made friends since this happened. I learned that friendship isn't guaranteed to be forever. You can be close like a sister except there is no certainty it will last. I have two sisters, one is gone and I don't speak to my other sister. Growing up my mother had so many friends. I had sisters and I didn't need female friends like my friends who have no sisters. My sister and I were very close, back then. Everything changes. I've learned you have to stop the craziness. It's good for you to do that.

Ghosting

The Journal of Social and Personal Relationships defines ghosting as a "dissolution strategy where the initiator ends all communication with the other person, ignoring attempts to reestablish the interaction." In a study, *Ghosting and Destiny: Implicit Theories of Relationships Predict Beliefs about Ghosting,* the authors found this form of separation is more common among women friends than among couples in romantic relationships. Women who are ghosted describe being shocked and shaken. In *Refinery 29,* "Our Expectations of Millennial Friendships Don't Prepare Us for the Reality," Poorna Bell writes, "Perhaps the hardest thing to acknowledge with any friendship is that sometimes relationships end, and friendships are no exception."

When someone is ghosted in the world of coupling, the more connected the lovers were, the more excruciating is the result. An article by Annie Tanasugarn, *What Really Drives Ghosting in Relationships,* can be applied to female friends as well. Tanasugarn notes that casual dating and online dating may end when a person ghosts the other person. The 'ghostee' can be 'confused, depressed or even traumatized.' In contrast, there are times when ghosting has validity. This would include a love relationship that has been harmful and ghosting creates a complete break from the person. If we apply this to a toxic female friendship, ghosting becomes a form of finale.

For example, Noreen, 29, a nutritionist living in a southern state with two small sons, has been ghosted by a good friend:

> This person, who was one of my best friends, had iced another mutual friend first. It was around the time when her grandfather died and she felt this person wasn't there for her. So it's not a total surprise that she cooled to me because she had done it to our friend a few years

> before. She'd get angry with someone and then she'd toss her out. It is sad because you can't get an old friend back if it goes like that. It feels like a hole is cut out. We had all these memories in common. She'll have memories but separate from mine. Her social circle has shrunk and she has a tumultuous dating life. It's all her loss. This one is about her and what she does to people.

Factoring in personality traits when it comes to the estranger or ghoster is understandable, as Noreen reports. However, what we see in this chapter are women who have taken the leap to estrange with ghosting as a tool.

Dalia, 35, working as a restaurant manager and living in the Midwest, is not bitter but relieved about her friendship that has ended:

> I had to disappear from this friend's life. If I saw her again we could only be acquaintances and I could only be polite. I wouldn't want to get to know her again. She was someone I thought I could count on in my life. Jealousy and competition do awful things. I have no expectations anymore. I don't need to reconnect at this point. I wish her well and her family. It is so hard to lose friends but in this case I had to do it. I think people change over time and have different needs in their lives. This friend turned on me and actually made up rumors. Whatever I confided was now cast out into the world. There was a lack of contact and lack of trust. I have imagined what I'd do if we somehow ran into each other. Since the day I opted out, neither of us reached out. It is so over.

Sabrina, 41, living in the Bay area where she works at a car dealership, is relieved that she and her friend no longer speak:

> I'm sure I'm the one who started it and then left. But it was in the works for a long time. She did terrible things but maybe she'd say I did too. Just like a break-up with a boyfriend. Should we have had some conversations about what was going on—probably, but we didn't. The experience taught me that a friendship that doesn't work is a lost cause. We're not enemies but not everyone you meet is going to be a lifelong bf. Today we each have our own circles and even back then, we did. It makes sense. The ghosting hurt, it wasn't easy, but I didn't have to have a conversation and the back and forth of it.

Preventative Measures

The degrees of disrepair that we've seen in this book are all too real. Ghosting or a blow up is the result of an uncomfortable friendship that has run its course. What is notable is how women of all ages are cutting their losses—and this is a departure from the recent past. Rather than avoid the decline of an important friendship, they are facing it and acting on it. They are assessing the pros and cons of what it would be like to never see the friend again. Even if it is their only recourse, there is a sense of liberation.

Which brings me to my friend Paulette. Over the years her deliberate actions against me became more apparent. During tough periods in our adult lives—divorce, work endeavors, career shifts, concerns for our children—we spent time together. Yet not during periods of prosperity for either one of us. I'd reach out—I did that too much—and there was no reply.

When we did reunite, she seemed somewhere between disinterested and angry if something was going well for me. I introduced her to someone in her field who I thought might help and she welcomed it. There was a short-lived window of gratitude, we were happy together. When this introduction didn't pan out, her resentment immediately churned up. As in the past, she stopped returning calls. That same sinking sense of self-doubt I'd known throughout the years, that it was my fault, resurfaced. Was any of her behavior any different than what she had done when we were together so long ago? What kind of trust could there be with this friend and why did I keep trying, why bother?

I began to compare my other close friendships to what I had or didn't have with Paulette. These women were genuine and constant, the comparison was obvious. There wasn't any rivalry or resentment, the friends were comfortable with themselves. The tide was turning, finally I was becoming less interested in sustaining a friendship with Paulette.

The same reaction is true for Denise, 53, an artist, married, with a stepdaughter, living in North Carolina. The variations with her friend had gone on and on:

> This woman couldn't be generous. It wasn't about relationship remorse but that friends and men were more desirable to her because I'd been involved with them.
>
> She was on a quest to find a man. We made dates and then she broke them. After a long list of these instances, where she went after anyone who mattered to me, I decided to stop being with her. Whatever she was doing, I was party to it, wasn't I? I told myself it was enough. About a year later she reached out and wanted to get together again. I think there was a situation where she didn't win, hadn't beat me out. I had introduced her

to a friend of mine and they got together a few times.
Then my friend realized how she could be and didn't
want to be with her. That surprised this friend and so her
decision was to rekindle our friendship and my decision
was to say never again.

I look back and remember there were ways I liked her
and respected how she handled things, her kids, elderly
relatives, balancing it all. She knew the ropes of being
single. She was between marriages and that motivated
her. There was a period when we felt we needed to see
each other. But she was both supportive and jealous of
me, even then.

Rebecca, 36, a full-time mother, living in Wisconsin, married with three children, has no regrets about her decision to sever ties with her friend:

> Recently I ran into this friend and there was no bad
> feeling but it is over. She's just not a friend I need in my
> orbit anymore. I'm not looking for what she wants and
> we are in different phases of life. I have children and
> they are a major game changer. I look at how I spend
> time compared to when she and I first met. We were
> single together and that's when we were closest. Now
> she is critical that I'm not working and judges me as a
> mother and wife. She is still in search of something big.
> She wants "the life" and that wouldn't mean mine. She
> is critical of how content I seem and says very nasty
> things to me. Is this really a friend? I finally had to face
> that and I let her know. I said it wasn't working. She was
> astonished. I knew on my side we couldn't get beyond it,
> there were too many parts that didn't work. I made the
> right choice.

Seventy percent of my interviewees report that leaving a friend is one of the most difficult actions they've ever taken. And while this chapter describes a variety of ways to break-up, fifty percent report they prefer a dwindling effect—the slow fade rather than a direct conversation. As we have seen, the estranger, no matter that she wants to leave the friendship, can be vague if confronted by the estrangee who might be devastated (although some are relieved, others are accepting). Interviewees report that because the friendship is disconcerting and unhealthy, estranging is a goal. Through breakups and ghosting, women become adept at estrangement and their lives are improved in the process.

Sister Balancing

This brings us to our next sister narrative, where two sisters were on a seesaw when it came to who distanced whom. Sydney, 45, who lives in Boston where she works for an online publication, tells us:

> I was the plainer sister. My sister, who is two years younger, was tall and very pretty from the start. By the time we were teenagers, everyone loved her. I saw it would never be easy. She had the right friends, the right clothes, the right look. Her boyfriends were like that too, just perfect. She had it made and I felt left behind. It didn't help that my mother favored her and gave her all her energy. My sister got married and I was her maid of honor but I could tell she wished it had been someone else. When her boys were born I wanted to spend time with them. My sister would agree but brushed me off if something better came along. Her husband is a surgeon

and her crowd was mostly wives/mothers who didn't work. I felt pushed to the side and unfavored. At holiday time I'd be invited or for the kids' birthday parties at first. As the years went on, my sister and her family included our parents for holidays. They'd travel over Thanksgiving or Christmas and wouldn't include me.

About a year ago my sister's husband wanted a divorce. My mother was calling and asking me to see her and to be supportive. She was falling apart, her friends were staying away from her. I got that. It was what she had done to me for years. I didn't have much sympathy because I'd been hurt and pushed aside for too long. So I didn't reach out, I wasn't there for her and finally we do not speak. It's a relief and my life is easier.

As revealed in this chapter, the dissolution of a deficient friendship or sister affinity can prove a successful move. Notwithstanding how drawn out or complicated the untangling becomes. A study by Blieszner, Ogletree and Adams, *Friendship in Later Life*, found that while friendships are important across a lifetime, that doesn't mean there aren't real issues between friends. We can apply this to women of all ages as they face their reality and in the process, reclaim themselves.

How we sequence the next steps:

Do you realize how much it has taken for you to end this friendship?

Once we have crossed the line to the other side, we often look back and realize how draining and time consuming it was with this friend.

Do you believe you could ever resurrect this relationship if an opportunity presented itself?

There might be some back and forth once the friendship is officially ended in some cases, while for others, the bond is severed and both parties have moved on.

When you reflect on the friendship do you feel nostalgic although you know it is for the best?

Missing the friend and what you shared is understandable. With new friends, new experiences and the passage of time, this feeling may lessen.

If you are the estranger, do you feel remorse or as if this is the right remedy?

Because female friendships are built on trust, intimacy and an emotional link, even as the **estranger**, one might second-guess her actions. What is notable is that by this stage of the friendship, it is also obviously the best decision.

Has your social life been affected by this estrangement?

There might be a ripple effect and estrangees often lament loss of a group as we have seen in previous chapters. However, the estrangee also knows there is power in the resolution of a harmful friendship, and over time can be accepting.

Do you feel more aware of what kind of female friendship will work for you?

Self-knowledge definitely comes with letting go of a friend who has brought (even if it didn't begin this way) anguish to your life. There is more caution going forward.

―――――

SHE SAID / SHE SAID

EXHIBIT H: Clarity

Selina and Diana

Here we are, near the completion of this book, with women who view a break-up with a female friend as essential. Still, there can be a nagging belief that friendships can be recalibrated and the heartache avoided. In this two-sided interview, Selina, 26, begins with a recap of a secure best friendship and a happy romantic life and how both failed her.

Selina

> Telling Diana everything made me feel safe. But that was before she made a terrible mistake, a deal breaker.
>
> •
>
> Diana and I were great friends for a very long time. Our families knew each other, as kids she went to my house or I went to hers for meals, for sleepovers. We went on vacations together, and to parties. This started in eighth grade and we were in college together. As students we were at each other's apartments, we had to be together. She knew my husband from when I met him. She knew everything, my deepest secrets and how I felt. After we graduated she knew how happy I was with Jacob, my boyfriend and that he and I were in love. We'd spend time together on weekends and we'd include Diana because

she was my best friend. What happened was I married Jacob and then he went off with Diana. I should have been more careful. I'm not sure what I was thinking.

As Selina's narrative unfolds, we nod, since ending up with your best friend's boyfriend/partner/husband, as evidenced in Chapter Seven, is one of the most egregious betrayals. While unfortunately it is a known scenario (as we have seen), in the Selina/Diana dyad, the attitude of both women and the result make it distinctive.

Telltale Signs

Today Selina, a medical school student living in Hartford, Connecticut, is comforted by the fact that she and Diana have no contact. Her sense of it was that there was no place for the friendship after the spectacle that ensued:

> I look back and search for how to have known. My family had money and Diana's did not have as much. Maybe that was a problem, maybe she was jealous. She had a nice boyfriend at the time, so he was also hurt by this. All four of us were involved and it was a bad thing. I ask myself why she would have done this to him.
>
> Jacob and I got divorced because of it. She was with him for a year and then they stopped being a couple. She betrayed me and broke my heart. She took too much from me.
>
> She made a mistake and then became pregnant. I couldn't easily forgive her. She had her baby and gave it up for adoption. Today, neither of us speaks with Jacob.

Selina would like to begin again with trustworthy people, but she feels she has no basis for this to be warranted.

> My goal is that I'll find love and a female friend I can trust. Since Diana, who was my bf, broke my trust it is harder to trust any girlfriend going forward. My mom was there for me and supported me spiritually. She wanted my life to go smoothly and she told me to let the grudge go, to start a new life. That was her suggestion. My sister also said the exact same thing. You have to move on, but it isn't something you can easily forget. I keep thinking that If I start another relationship, it could happen again. So now I am afraid. That Diana betrayed me so much is very painful. Someone so close to you can destroy your life. It's such a terrible wound."

Friends versus Spouses

Selina had decided that Jacob was not as culpable as Diana and that he is not to be held accountable on the same level. The loss of Diana in her life was such a serious blow that whatever occurred with Jacob was overtaken by those machinations. Notably, Selena was much more invested in Diana and the turmoil of their friendship:

> I can forgive Jacob although he also made a mistake. But compared to my best friend, Diana, it isn't as painful.
> I wish him well, but for my best female friend, it was worse than what Jacob did. I do not want to be near her ever. She would do it again and I want to protect myself. I will avoid her as much as I can and try to stop thinking of what

she did. Before it happened, I never imagined something like this. I miss the good moments, the good memories when we were happy together and helped each other so much. If I had to blame anyone, I'd blame Diana first before Jacob. She saw what she was doing and knew how we were best friends. She destroyed my life and she fooled me. I expected a lot from her and this is what she did. When I compare us, she was more mature than I was. She advised me and then look at her. I had high expectations.

I just want to fix my life and start a new one where no one knows all this pain. I'm working on myself to get it right.

Diana

I have so much guilt, maybe Selena will move on and I'll feel better. I feel bad about the baby too. Maybe Selina will adopt a child. Maybe this will all get better.

•

Selina and I were best friends from high school and went to the same university. That's where we met Jacob who married Selina. But what happened after this is part of the story too. For four years Selina had a problem because she can't have kids and it was a source of tension between them. I knew everything that was going on. I was really in the middle of it.

Entangled

Diana, 28, lives in New Haven, Connecticut where she works in an accounting firm. She is single and has no children. She and Selina have not spoken for three years. As the situation unfolded, she has felt alone and deeply regretful for what happened. She has felt unsupported and blamed without back up coming in any direction:

> What happened is that Jacob loved me but it could never be separated from how he was married to my best friend. But I knew it and also knew how complicated it was. He was doing well with work. He had a big job with the same company where I work and he wanted a family. I felt horrible every day. Selina would want to get together, Jacob would want to meet, it was the same day, same hour they were both suggesting.
>
> It was like I was stuck in this life where I had to act like everything was okay and Selina and I were best friends without my big secret. She didn't know and it was what I carried around. I had strong feelings for Jacob and if he hadn't been her husband, it would have been right for me. He wanted a family and it was hanging over them, they were a couple with a problem. Outside of that, there was what Jacob and I had together.
>
> I know it isn't the only story like this but it felt like that.

Decomposing

While Diana was attempting to manage her life with Selina and Jacob, Selena reached out. Diana said she was too busy at work. In some manner, this was the turning point in terms of the friendship. She made excuses because she couldn't face Selina. The relationship with Jacob was heating up and her priorities had shifted.

CHAPTER EIGHT | 214

> Things were getting harder to handle. Jacob and I sneaked out when we could. He and I lied to be together. When we went on a vacation that was part business, it changed, that's when it became romantic. Selina didn't know. Jacob said he wanted to marry me. We talked about it. When we were travelling without her, he proposed to me. I admired him, he was ambitious and very handsome. Their marriage was not good. I told him I couldn't marry him because he was married to my best friend. I thought that Selina suspected something and it made me feel very uncomfortable. She and I were too connected for this.
>
> What went on during this business trip should have been no big deal. Except, unfortunately on that trip I became pregnant. What was I going to say to my best friend, Selina? How I saw it was that Jacob had to break up with her because she couldn't have children and he wanted this so much. I had to tell him to tell Selina what was going on. I knew she had to know. It was a mess. Jacob kept saying he loved me. But we didn't end up together and so I gave the baby up for adoption. Selina stopped speaking to me. She and Jacob split up. Neither of us stayed in touch with him, that I know about. No one sees Jacob. It is about the two of us, Selina and I come first.

Although the friends have not spoken since this occurred, Diana believes the friendship needs to heal and continue.

> We aren't best friends anymore, because the faith was broken. Selina does not keep grudges but she was very upset and does not want to be in touch with me. I know what I did and I wonder if Selina can find a place in her heart to forgive me. We were so close, such good friends.

The friendship was the main factor. There is so much that was lost and I accept that. If she won't speak with me, I understand. We both need to start fresh, separately, have good lives again.

Can This Friendship Be Saved?

The acute emotional injury that occurred in this friendship is obvious. This causes us to question what level of nurturance and support ever existed between Selina and Diana. Simone de Beauvoir, author of *The Second Sex*, has been quoted as saying "Women's feelings rarely rise to genuine friendship." While we know the standard is that we achieve authentic bonds with our women friends, in *Estranged, we* understand our ability to remove ourselves from a friendship that is destructive. Because women engage in self-disclosure and confide in other women, we can assume that Diana knew details of Selina's quest to have a child with Jacob. To that end, what happened between her and Jacob is a double betrayal—first she was involved with her best friend's husband and following that she conceived his child.

In Fanny Lalot's essay "The Unkindest Cut of All: A Quantitative Study of Betrayal Narratives," betrayal is defined as a breach of trust that includes willful violations such as deception and disloyalty. Such maneuvers transpire only with someone we know and believe in—as found in the narratives throughout this book. What is most disturbing is the deliberate aspect of Diana's choices and the woe it caused Selina.

Which brings us to estrangement as a solution, one that will free both women to begin anew and recover from pain that was inflicted and endured. For Selena, there are lessons learned. The decisions she has made are a form of self rescue and affirmation.

CHAPTER NINE

Successful Estrangements

- Have you noticed how time feels easier without this friend?
- Has your energy improved without her?
- Do you talk with others about how this friendship has played out?
- Are you looking forward to new beginnings?
- Do you feel this is a personal success?

If you are affirmative in your answers, you have achieved a fortunate estrangement.

> After too much time invested in this friend, you have not only moved away from making excuses, but are letting go. Your previous thought and decision to tolerate whatever played out—that went on for months or years—no longer hold up, Like telling yourself you share a history, there is a loyalty factor, this friend needs you, your mothers were friends. The idea of forgiving her for an egregious

deed and that her jealousy can be overlooked, has all dissolved. There have been too many times when the friendship was painful and disappointing. Or worse, your friend has issues and you cannot be her co-dependent. Or her values are not yours as they once were, or the trust between you has eroded. How about when this friend demoralized you in front of other friends, or gave away your secrets?

Sure, what is described above is familiar and you have been the long-suffering friend, as have many women. The guilt that surrounded leaving this friend was so great that you actually backpedaled at times. First you would say to anyone who would listen, I've had enough, I'm not going to be abused emotionally. I'm not going to allow this friend to hurt me another time. I'm not her doormat. Yet you were and it was clouding your vision. You weren't able to leave her, despite what you knew about her and about yourself. Besides, we live in a culture that endorses female friendship and remains a patriarchy—meaning women need to buoy one another. You couldn't bail, it would be a failure. We are meant to cherish our girlfriends while living with mixed messages on a daily basis. On the one hand, we're brought up to believe that we need our female friends and wouldn't be the same without them. On the other, the media delights in depicting rivalry, betrayal, deception and viciousness among women. What could be juicier than battling women friends on screen or on social media, as long as it isn't your life?

Today your reality has changed and you have taken charge. You have reevaluated the past five times you were with this friend and admit it isn't what a friendship should be. This is heady stuff—already you are lighter and smile more. You have discarded the fear of days with her, replacing it with the hope of being with sympathetic, caring friends. You as the estranger have successfully estranged!

The Brink

In Chapter Eight there is evidence that: a) after many situations and accumulated efforts or b) an event with serious repercussions, a friendship is over. In this chapter we consider estrangements that work in our favor. Now that we have been through the ups and downs of a friendship on the rocks, we're ready to make the cut. Women have overcome indecision and doubt and are prepared to estrange. This applies to any category identified in the past chapters. We have witnessed breakups as well as second attempts and earnest efforts at Plan B with a close friend. In this chapter the friendship is on the line and the estranger has hit her threshold. A bold, successful estrangement is the solution.

As Philip Lopate views it in his essay "On the Death of Friendship," the error is in our assumption that we will remain friends without a fixed limit. He writes "... the waning of a friendship should be no more a mystery than mortality itself." This brings us to my questionnaire at the end of the book. What I learned is that 79.28 percent of a diverse group of over one hundred women believed that being estranged from a friend has been a positive step.

Consider Adele, 43, living in the southwest where she works as a real estate broker:

> I remember how long it took me to leave this friend and how upset I was about it. But I needed to do it, there was

no reason to stay. I am closer with other people now and wouldn't have been so open to other friends had it not been for ending the friendship. I have a new friend where we do fun things together and we have more in common than with the ex-friend. I'm more exposed because of the breakup and more open because of it too. She and I did not know each other as I thought we did. She had a façade and I didn't really understand her. She cared so little about me and my life. It was about what I could do for her. What's so strange is how long I worried about leaving her and how glad I am without her.

Jessica, 30, living in Milwaukee where she is a freelance writer, left her best friend over a betrayal:

I was close with two friends and introduced them. They became too close to include me and they sort of kicked me out. After deciding not to be with both of them, they were sad I think. I heard they stopped talking to each other. I don't care about that. The more important friend and I went our separate ways. I wanted nothing to do with her. She would call and I wouldn't take the call for months. Then one day I did pick up and she apologized, she went on and on. She wanted things to go back to how it was and I said no because of what she had done. It wasn't forgivable. But I said okay to her apology. Today if we run into each other, we'll say hi and be polite. But there is nothing ever to be shared as it was. That's over and I'm relieved. I'd had enough.

Sarah, 54, lives in Washington State, where she manages a convenience store. She has a daughter who is 34 and just had a baby:

I look back and I would not be friends with this woman again. It would remind me of what she did and what it took to let her go. At some point since, I've missed her and then I remember what she did and how she did it. It had to do with my family, let's say she's someone who got between us. I'm not ready to make friends with more women. I've reached a point where meeting people is too hard. She and I were close in a way I'm not with most girlfriends. What happened was nauseating for me, until I stopped seeing her. That made me stronger.

Isolated

No one wants to be alone as interviewees explained when I asked why they stayed in negative, unrewarding friendships. In June of 2020, the *Today Show* ran an online piece about how during the pandemic couples were spending more time together and feeling lonely all the same. The salient point was that a wife's initial level of loneliness had a direct effect on her husband too. The remedy was that women should interact with their female friends and sustain the rapport. Female bonds (healthy ones) proved beneficial and staved off feeling secluded. As Stephanie Cacioppo, a neuroscientist, writes in her book, *Wired for Love*, "The tricky thing about loneliness is that, to some extent, it's self-reinforcing and even self-fulfilling."

This can be a precept of estrangement, where the decision is sound and women feel intrepid for choosing it, but there is the empty space where the friend and the friendship existed.

For example, Allie, 33, living in Wyoming, is an estranger. She works part time at an employment agency and has a young daughter and a partner:

> Leaving work full time made me feel isolated and so does not going out ever with my friends because of the baby. I wasn't really at work except as a fill in person. I began to feel stuck and I leaned on this one friend, we'd been close from when we were kids. I thought we understood each other and I'd feel less alone. My whole world changed. I had a baby and a partner. We'll probably get married. I look back and realize this friend was mean-spirited. She told my partner Sam about me, all these negative things I'd confided like how it was hard to be alone at home, how a baby was boring. I thought Sam was going to leave me he was so angry. I decided to stop the friendship. I wanted no part of it. As soon as I did, I knew I'd be okay.

On the other side of estrangement is Laurie, 24, a graduate student, living in upstate New York. Recently she became the estrangee when her best friend shut her out. The desolation of being without this friend is palpable:

> Neither of us is willing to face the other and we don't talk or communicate on social media. I remember the things we did together and how it mattered to us. We'd hang out, go shop, listen to music, see our friends. I don't speak to her, but she started it. She just let me go and never said why. There's this empty space where she used to be. I'm trying to get used to it. I feel very different without her. I replay all these times that we spent together and I can't figure out what it was. Maybe that she wants to be with someone and doesn't want me hanging around. Maybe she wants to get back at me for something. But we were never unkind to one another, we were never mean. I think she became sick of me and so I'm without her.

Goals

In Hyde and Kling's essay. "Women, Motivation, and Achievement" achievement motivation is defined as "the desire to accomplish something of value or importance through one's own efforts and to meet standards of excellence in what one does." To me, this sums up how women approach their relationships as well as their careers, finances, and mothering. We are goal oriented and determined. But at what price with a messy, untrustworthy friend?

Two novels come to mind where the estrangees' behaviors are so egregious that we can't help but root for estrangement. In *Keep Your Friends Close* by Paula Daly, Eve is the bad friend who wants to have her friend Natty's entire life, including her husband and home. In *Precious Thing* by Colette McBeth, Rachel and Clara are friends from when they were teenagers. We don't know whom to trust as they compete for the best life. Estrangement might benefit both characters in this book.

Friendship is high on the list of importance for women, no matter what age or stage we're at. The ideal is for friendship to be a win/win. The argument as we have seen, is that it might not be an achievement and offer a reward, but in fact the opposite. A goal for women is to have a network of friends they can count on. Today, as we wake up to the truth of some of our friendships, letting go is a goal as well. This proves another sort of reward in terms of self-care and self-awareness.

For example, MaryAnn, 47, living in Boise, Idaho, where she has two middle school sons, views what happened with her friend of fifteen years as a wake-up call and a 'moving goal line.'

> My friend and I started this social hour friend group together and built it up. That was very important to both of us. Basically she wanted to run it and so did I. We

traded off and co-hosted for years but after a while, I saw that she wasn't happy. She wanted my position to be hers, in other words, for me to disappear. It was a lot of effort—we had to find different venues to meet, increase attendance, all that. During Covid we kept it going with virtual meetings. After that we took office space and worked there. After a while I knew she wanted not just this position I had, but other parts of my life. I was getting uncomfortable. I decided to leave the friendship because it made me anxious. The times we'd had fun together were long gone.

I have no regrets going forward without her. It forced me to have better friends. I have really good friends now. But after this, new friends make me cautious. I learned so much from our separation, like how to tell when it isn't for real.

Other women report friendship ruptures from both sides, that of estranger and estrangee. Albeit they've put tremendous energy into these bonds, they are hitting their limit.

For Emily, 34, living in Boston and working in data analytics, her college best friend's life strategy has soured their friendship:

This friend won't spend time with anyone who doesn't get her closer to her goal of a husband, kids, high earning work, a social life. She only wants people in her world who fit in. I suppose she dropped me out because I'm not useful to her. What could I contribute? But I also left her because I don't care about her plans and how she puts them into play. What we never did was talk about it, instead this happened over time. I'm a little resentful because I don't respect her at this stage. But I'm not sorry for a minute that we don't talk anymore.

Heather, 69, living in a retirement community in Arizona, describes being tossed out of her tennis league once she was widowed:

> After my husband died, a few longtime friends stopped putting me in the games. I wasn't part of a couple so I didn't fit in. What I was looking for had changed. I wanted to be with women who were also alone and not be some third wheel at dinner. That's what they do here—if you're divorced or widowed, at first your friends with husbands or partners take you to dinner and after that they dump you. I had a plan to join a widow's group but they're ungenerous about letting someone in who no one knew. So one good friend dropped me from the married group and a new friend dropped me from the singles group when I met my boyfriend. I'm happy to be without these friends.

Watershed

While some friendships have a long history and others are more recent, those on the receiving end of an overt split have mixed emotions, including rejection, denial and regret. We've explored the triggers that drive women to abandon a friendship: divisive outsiders, dangerous behaviors, opposing values, ranking/exclusion, disparagement, lies and secrets, jealousy, a breach of trust and the trauma that ensues. If your friend has done something flagrant—such as in Exhibit D when Nicole lied to Sandy and shut her out completely and in Exhibit E when Sarah spilled May Lynn's paternity secret and ruined life as she knew it—the estrangement isn't questioned.

That would mean both the estranger and estrangee feel the seismic shift in their friendship as the result of the estrangee's behavior.

Gigi, 37, lives in Jackson, Mississippi, where she works for a pharmacy chain. Presently she is engaged. Her experience leads us in another direction:

> My mother has several sisters and a few important women friends. I noticed if someone gets in her way, she cuts them off. She has learned to curb her natural inclination to forgive other's mistakes and encouraged me to make a decision about this one friend. I have used my mother as a model. She's very young looking and thin and has not always been well treated by other women.
>
> I had to face this was not a good friend, and we were going nowhere. We were the same at thirty as we'd been together as teenagers. She was jealous of me and convinced I was jealous of her. She always thought people were envious of her looks, including me. In high school, there was a guy who liked me and she ended up sleeping with him. I stayed with her because even though it was a betrayal, he wasn't my boyfriend. This friend wanted whatever I had and anyone I had. I had to stop feeding the dragon. The last two years I stopped going home for holidays to avoid her and our circle of friends. Finally I dropped everyone in that group to escape her. I'm proud of myself.

Like Gigi, Andi, 50, living in Rapid City, South Dakota, had a dysfunctional friendship with one of her closest female friends for years. Andi has a daughter in college and lives with a long-term partner:

> I have a friend who has always been impossible to deal with. When we were young mothers we were friends and it made sense. I overlooked a lot of what she did. She always thought she was right and had to prove it. She was very self-centered and if it wasn't about her, she wasn't interested. But lately, as the world changes and I look at it differently, I know I don't need to put up with her. She has done some vile things and it has added up. Here we are, years after we first became friends, and I am finished. After Covid and what happened to people, I still don't want this pebble in my shoe. This friend has no idea of how I feel. What frustrated me was that at first I didn't have a complete peace of mind with this. I didn't know how to avoid news of her. I had to make a decision to be apart and remind myself I have not really dealt with it in decades. I wanted to and I didn't do it. Now I've separated and I'm finally putting it to rest.

Tiffany, 44, living in Atlanta, works in Human Resources and is single. She has no children:

> In retrospect what happened fourteen years ago was important. I had just turned thirty and my patience was short for people who were not good for me. I dismissed this friend and her boyfriend at the time. I was raised by my grandparents. I knew her because she was in the same neighborhood growing up. We were in grade school and high school together. We had issues from the start and our friends rallied around us when there were problems in the past. I knew I needed to grow and change back then, it wasn't an easy time. I tried to discuss it with this friend. I wanted to explain how I felt about our friendship. But if the conversation didn't include her,

she had no attention for it. She didn't understand even though she thought she was the smartest person in the room. When I moved to Atlanta, she was still back home and I felt like I'd left her there. We had been like sisters, gone to proms, parties, life experiences were shared. Our lives were entwined. We were sisters to each other. In our mid-twenties, she was in a new relationship and he did not like me. It made it hard for us and I knew it would not work out for her. I saw what kind of person he was. She couldn't hear me. It came between us.

This friend and I had a fall-out but I wanted to explain things. I didn't want to give up on her. She wasn't popular. People wondered why we were friends. I had to admit it was time to separate. I stopped speaking to her and cut it off. No calls, texts, emails, it was difficult because family friends interfered. It was exactly like a divorce, the way people took sides.

She kept trying to be in touch. She was possessive of me when we broke up and she was possessive before. I knew what she wanted was to prove it was not her fault that we were over. I'd made up my mind. Things were accumulating and added to my decision to leave. It knew it would be difficult. Had I grown up enough to leave, I asked myself. The answer was yes. She was not going to change ever and staying as we were was not an option for me.

Absolved

What distinguishes the friendships in this chapter is that they do end. There isn't a hiatus and then a reunion or a confessional followed by an attempt to go forward one more round. These decisions are about positive estrangements, where the friends are better off apart and both estranger and estrangee know this deep down. Novels and film that show us loaded pasts include the three-way friendship in Lauren Mechling's *How Could She*. In this story, nothing is what it seems as old time friends realize the price of glamour, self-confidence and backbiting. In Jennifer Weiner's *Big Summer*, two friends, Daphne, the historical sidekick to Drue, the popular one, haven't spoken in six years. When Drue asks Daphne to be in her wedding, a revisiting of their shared past emerges. The classic film *Stage Door* (1937) is about a developing friendship after an initial meeting filled with insults and competition.

"We see what we want to see," therapist Donald Cohen tells us. "These friendships are about being understood and supported. When they don't work out that way, it is a surprise. That can be very challenging and very serious. Women who feel brave will leave the friend and feel they've been acquitted."

There are women who have realized early on the ups and downs of female bonds and have protected themselves and honed their skills for exiting. Consider Nora, 54, a freelancer who grew up in Scandinavia and presently lives in Charleston, South Carolina:

> I do not have problems with any of my female friends presently. When we were young, there were incidents. The first was when I dated someone and my best friend was interested in him. We were in our twenties and it destroyed the friendship. The situation was not important to her but it was to me and I wasn't going to let it go. While it is definitely in the past, it was only years later that we talked about it. This is my best friend and she still is today. What happened was she was interested in him and he was not into her. It became an issue for certain. We moved past it because it wasn't a serious

> relationship, or else we couldn't have gone forward. But
> had it been a man who mattered to me—or a business
> opportunity, or a rescue dog I had my eyes on—it
> would have been another story. I would have ended the
> friendship on principle.

Lourdes, 56, living in Washington State, where she works in the beverage industry, views her ability to leave a soured friendship as necessary:

> I grew up one of five sisters and it was very intense in
> terms of female connections. I was very close to my
> female friends and to my sisters. We were loyal. When
> something went wrong, it was very upsetting. My sisters
> could be competitive with each other, but not my friends.
> I had lots of friends growing up. There was one girl in
> sixth grade who was a mean girl. She became the leader
> of my group and my mother had to listen to the stories of
> what she did. My mother was always sympathetic. One
> day this leader of the group told the other girls not to
> talk to me; we were only twelve. It really stuck with me.
> It made me realize how it can be among females. Decades
> later, this taught me to leave friends—I've had two—
> when it gets rough. I don't stay around because I know
> what will happen. I can leave a best friend easily. I won't
> get involved with the meanness and the lies.

Sister Act

Several sisters reported that despite their longing to be close to their sister, it wasn't manageable. For this chapter I've chosen Tina's story. She is 42, living in Vermont and working as a medical administrator. She is married with two sons. Her struggles with her sister, who is two years older, have existed since she can remember:

> My sister and I have always looked alike. When we were little, our mother even dressed us in these matching outfits. I think she hated it even when she was seven and I was five.
>
> We always had very different styles. I was the one who always agreed and would do whatever we were supposed to do. My sister didn't care, she did what she wanted and she had some kind of power by doing that. By the time we were in high school it was very difficult to be the younger sister. We were mistaken for each other, which really annoyed her. We were compared constantly and I always felt like I wasn't measuring up. We could never confide in each other and we couldn't double date with the boyfriends in high school or college. I asked a few times and she said no, it wasn't happening. I wanted to share clothes and again, she said no.
>
> We ended up in the same college and I don't think that was a good idea. And then we both married young and had our first children about the same time. I was upset about her all the time, I wanted to be close to her, but she set it up so we were competitive. She extended it to our husbands, who were successful but to different degrees. She also wanted our mother to choose her and she'd reach out to her, ask her to spend time. When my mother wanted me and my kids to be included, she said no.
>
> The fact that we live in the same town has made it worse. We've had to choose friends who did not overlap. It was like you were my friend or you were her friend and that made it very hard for me. She even controlled

who was left for me to be with. I wanted her to be my friend first, I thought about it every day. Twice in the last twenty years my sister decided to talk to me and act like we were close sisters. But it never lasted, and she just distanced herself again.

Every year our mother invited both of us and our families to her house for holidays. My sister told her that if I came, she would not come. This was so unfair to our parents, but it was also about trying to fix things. I suppose no one could fix it and in the end my mother came to our house for part of the day and to my sister's for part of the day. Now my husband and I take our kids away for most holidays so I don't have to feel so sad.

I would say that my sister always saw me as a threat and that made her unkind to me. If we did run into each other at overlapping school events or sometimes at friends or cousins, it was very awkward. I tried to get our kids together through our mother, without either of us there but she objected to that too. Recently my sister landed a very good job and I thought maybe that would make her happier, maybe friendlier to me? But it didn't work out that way.

The last few months I've decided that I don't want to reach out anymore. I've hit my limit. Our mother will have to decide how to spend her time with each of us. I know my sister always wanted more time with her as if she could win that part of the game too. I have decided to let it go. I am facing how she makes me feel, what it has done to me and I'm stopping it all. I don't want to be with her, I'm accepting that my sister is not in my life. I am the one saying it's over. Mostly, I'm proud of myself for finally saying enough.

How we enter the arena:

Is there a sense you are a warrior to have estranged from a complicated friendship?

We can't underestimate how counterintuitive it is to leave a friendship that has meaning. However, estranging because the environment is detrimental to our well-being is reasonable.

Would you share your news of your estrangement with friends and family or keep it to yourself?

Women feel judged in their interactions and a sense of failing at a relationship is one of the 'heavies.' Yet as we have witnessed in the women's stories, leave-taking is a form of self-protection and liberating.

Are you going against your personality by making this break with a friend?

Part of waking up is realizing we've remained in these relationships for too long. We have to do better at it, despite that it goes against our usual pattern, as interviewees have shown us.

Whether you are the estranger or the estrangee, have there been benefits as a result of the estrangement?

It is interesting to note how many interviewees are relieved on either side of the dissolved friendship. There is tremendous comfort in having taken this step.

Are there lessons learned in having spent time with a friend you end up leaving?

The idea that we learn from our mistakes applies here. Hopefully we won't repeat our pattern with the next 'best' friend and our antennae will be up. While some women have said they are hesitant to start anew and trust is an issue, when they do, it is with hard earned wisdom.

Whether estranger or estrangee, do you recognize what transpired in this friendship?

Being able to take responsibility for what you contributed to the friendship matters. How else can we be authentic in the next go-round? It is a form of self-recognition.

SHE SAID / SHE SAID

EXHIBIT I: **Acceptance**

Ilse and Bettie

For our final two-sided interview, we'll look at a friend who betrays her friend on several levels. As we've read, most of the friendships have one specific issue. For example in Chapter Two, it is a friend engaged in dangerous behavior, in Chapter Three it is the friend with dissimilar values, in Chapter Five, it is the hyper-critical friend. In the following pages the price of acceptance is high. Let's begin with Ilse, 30, whose belief in Bettie's loyalty disintegrated over time.

Ilse

My sister did not like Bettie. She never thought she was a good friend. My mother told me to be on the lookout, to watch my back.

•

My ex-best friend has been in my life for a long time. That's what makes what happened so much harder. We worked at our first job after college together. I was the one who told her about a position there and she got in. It was at a real estate company, and we had the same supervisor. I had always introduced Bettie to everyone, I always shared with her. She knew the people in life, my boyfriend who became my fiancé, and my cousin. She once slept with my boyfriend and swore it was a mistake. I let it go and stayed with both of them. She knew how much I wanted to succeed at this company. I told her all about it and the strategy I had. But she messed with my plans and went to our superior acting like these were her ideas. While she was doing that she invited my cousin to dinner without me. I was pretty offended. I was about to confront her when my sister told me she had seen Bettie walking out of a Starbucks with my fiancé. It could have been a coincidence except it had this sickening feeling about Bettie, she was out to take what's mine.

If Ilse's narrative is familiar, especially the part about Bettie being spotted with Ilse's fiancé, her ability to estrange is the headline here. We've seen a number of cases of best friends where one ends up with the other's partner/husband. Ilse, however, is concerned with the whole picture and Bettie's lack of boundaries. That her fiancé was spotted with Bettie is another reminder of her friend's nature. It is an overall disrespect that so disturbs her.

Zero Tolerance

Recently Ilse moved to Lexington, Kentucky and is taking a course requirement to become a Pilates instructor. This divergent path from the real estate business that mattered so much to her is a deliberate decision.

> After what happened with Bettie, I wanted to start fresh. She and I had shared an apartment after college. I remember back then she was flirting with my fiancé, who was then my boyfriend. I knew I had to keep her away and at the same time my focus was on the office. There was an opening for a junior position, and I knew I could grow there. I told Bettie, who also applied and was hired and it was my fault for giving her the info. Then I ask myself, wouldn't she have wormed in anyway? It was fine while we were on the same team at work but then she was promoted and I wasn't. I was devastated at first. I couldn't even look at Bettie, She was acting like it was a coincidence, it just sort of happened to her, not that she was all over my future position and knew my ideas. While we were both working at this company, for two years after she got the better job, I had to still be friendly. There were too many paths that crossed, too many friends in common and I had to go forward. I showed up for work smiling like it was okay. I sat down in my cubicle while Bettie had a real office. She had the job I wanted and had worked for. I was furious and hurt at the same time. How else could I get through but to tone it down? I wouldn't be alone with her. I couldn't stand it.
>
> I spoke to my sister and my mother. They told me Bettie had made a mistake and to forgive her. I said it wasn't the job, it was that she was my best friend and this is how she operated. I couldn't get over it. It has

made me think differently about trusting new girlfriends. Going forward, I wouldn't let any of my friends know about something at work that opens up. I'm switching careers because of what she did. Now I know I wouldn't introduce any of my friends to my work connections or to a man I was with. I wouldn't even share my friends with anyone again. I had to leave and luckily my fiancé understood.

Self Protection

By the time I moved away and had left the company, Bettie was eyeing someone else's husband and dissing everyone in the office. As if she had become the boss. I decided she was a fake friend. She wanted to ruin my life or maybe someone else's, whoever was next. I realized I had no choice but to cut Bettie out because she would just keep taking from me. I moved on but right afterward I felt awful. Today I'm happier and plan to be married next year. I don't want to know about Bettie. My mother was right when she warned me. She had said we were both raised the same way but didn't do the same thing.

I have made a new woman friend who is trustworthy, a good person. She is married with children. I can count on her. I've learned to know who your friends are, and what loyalty is. Bettie will never be my friend again. I blame her. She had a negative motive toward me and went after whatever she could. I should not have been interacting with her for so long. She and I have gone our separate ways. I was the one who stopped talking to her.

Bettie

We have been friends since eighth grade. Ilse would say it changed when we worked for the same company, I'd say it was before that. Ilse wouldn't believe anything I say in my defense anyway.

•

Ilse and I during college fought first about our boyfriends and later about work. I decided to get my real estate license because she did. When she went to this management company—I followed her. She seemed sure what to do and I wasn't certain. At first she seemed fine with my being hired. Later she was angry and accused me of taking her job. That isn't what happened, our boss chose and he wanted me. Just like her boyfriend liked me better, that's how it happened.

No Limits

Bettie, 30, lives in Indiana and works in real estate. She has a young child and is presently single. She believes that Ilse suspected without knowing that she became involved with Ilse's then boyfriend:

> What started everything with Ilse is what happened with Ilse's boyfriend when we were in school and about to graduate. She was all set and I was trying to find a job and feeling very pressured by my family. First she gave me the name of the real estate company where she was going to work. So how could I confess that I'd been with her boyfriend one night, that one thing had led to another. I had wanted to tell her right away but I didn't

for quite some time. I couldn't hide it any longer so I did. By then I'd already been interviewed by the office she told me about. She didn't seem mad at first but after a while she stopped talking to me about anything that mattered. She became really angry. I apologized to her and said it wasn't my intention with her boyfriend. She was mad that I'd kept it inside for too long. She felt that her boyfriend and I had been deceiving her and taking her for a fool. She told me she was over me and I asked her to stay in the friendship. We were about to work together in our real jobs out of school. I even had my mother talk to her, begging her to still be my friend. The guilt was torture for me.

Heedful

Once Ilse was aware of Bettie's M.O., Bettie knew the friendship was on a slippery slope. Her intention was to salvage the relationship and so she was cautious at work and in her romantic life. She hoped that nothing would bother Ilse and that her ambition about her career would be understandable to Ilse, who had the same view of it:

> Ilse and I were together at work and put in the same group. So we saw each other but we didn't do anything social, she wouldn't. She gave off this cold vibe and I tried to ignore it. I'm not sure what I would have done about the friendship if it hadn't been that we were together at work. I admit I always wanted the same clothes and style as she had. We went to the same gym for classes and we knew the same people from work, so we were together

but not best friends anymore. It was miserable. Ilse seemed bothered by it too. It wasn't only on my side.

About six months into being at this company, our supervisor told me I was getting a raise and better position. I was so happy and so nervous at the same time—I knew Ilse would be furious. She'd brought me into this career, she'd guided me and I was going to step over her. Not by my decision but by our boss's decision. I wondered if I deserved it, if it wasn't worth being here because Ilse was always fuming. One day after work she confronted me and said I wanted anything that she cared about, that there was nothing left of our friendship because I'd taken it all.

Justification

I tried to apologize right then and afterward I kept trying to reach her and apologize, to say I'd never meant to do any of it. She wouldn't speak to me, she didn't answer my texts or emails or calls. I think I knew how it was for her, I was benefitting from her choice of where to work, I had slept with her old boyfriend years ago. Eventually she left the company. I heard she was moving. I asked my mother to find out because our mothers knew each other a little. We were from the same town and same background. My mother said it was true, she'd decided to move to Kentucky. Her fiancé was from there. There was no message from her in any form and I kept hoping she would let go of everything and we could be friends again. But she totally iced me and I know she can't forgive me. I don't blame her for why but it would have been nice to have talked it through. I know we won't be speaking again.

Can This Friendship Be Saved?

While romantic love may hold out an air of mystery, when it comes to our intimate female friendships, we want to be known and sustained. It makes us safe, we are on steady ground. These are our expectations and our hopes and in the twenty-first century, the collective norm. According to a study by Ingo, Mize and Pratarelli, "Female Intrasexual Competition: Toward an Evolutionary Feminist Theory," "females evolved an indirect way of aggressing toward one another." The authors also reference "gossip and backstabbing" as methods for women to "effectively eliminate a rival." On screen we've seen examples including *Legally Blonde*, where Elle, played by Reese Witherspoon, arrives at Harvard Law School and the other female students initially ostracize her, *Cinderella*, (book and film) a classic, features the wicked stepmother and her daughters mistreating Cinderella. This is only because she presents as the competition in their quest to ensnare the prince. In *Bridgerton* (book and film) set in regency times, social standing for young women could only be won through marriage. The competition was fierce with limited available men and beauty as a measure.

As we apply this to modern day scenarios, Ilse regards Bettie's actions as reason to not remain friends. Ilse's pathway is obvious, she estranges from her friendship with Bettie. As estranger she has made a clean break that is imperative for her to go forward.

Since Bettie is aware of what she has done and somewhat remorseful, she recognizes Ilse will not be her friend anymore. Nonetheless, as estrangee, she wants a chance to explain herself. Coming from opposing sides, these two friends have differing definitions of what constitutes betrayal. Bettie is defensive more than repentant and her need to have what essentially belongs to Ilse dovetails with female aggression, as cited above. Thus, estrangement is the answer and an appropriate step.

EPILOGUE

Owning Our Decisions

Over time researching, interviewing and writing, I have been reminded of why this topic intrigued me from the start. Estrangement among female friends is an ongoing and complex pursuit—one that hasn't readily been identified or discussed. There isn't enough support or acknowledgment for women whose friendships are intensely troubled or have ended. Instead the success of our female bonds—friends and sisters alike—has been emphasized. The leave-taking hasn't been prioritized and even today we may feel judged by the outcome.

This is despite the determination of those who estrange because 1) these friendships are expected to flourish, 2) the loss of the friend is acute and 3) female estrangement has not been a prescriptive norm. What we're hearing in the voices of the women is relief. They are free from the burden of an arduous, negative situation.

Rather than repairing our issues with a friend or enduring an unbalanced relationship—where one friend feels inadequate and the other is too powerful—estrangement is a brave leap into closing out the friendship. Estrangement is the recognition of being better off without this friend.

Consider the following women who have achieved this:

Renata, 41, a math tutor, living in South Carolina, is perplexed that her best friend has estranged from her. She also takes responsibility for what she has done:

> I've been part of this tight community and we know everyone's business. You would never cross any of the women, it wouldn't work. That's why I can't believe my friend stopped speaking to me. We're known as best friends and no one else could get as close as we are. Then I pissed her off. I wasn't able to help out with her elderly mother one time. I should have been honest but instead I made up an excuse. She won't forgive me, no matter what I say or do. She was the one who always told me what to do and then I didn't come through. Mostly there are long days without her. It's miserable. When I think of her side, and I try to, I realize she is finished with me. What I did really pushed a button. It all adds up, the friendship is over.

For Becca, 60, a physician living in Maryland, leaving a friend who had changed completely made sense:

> I was very close to a friend from medical school so this was a long while ago. My friend got married while I felt very single and that caused some barriers right away. I don't think I fit in with her life anymore. The man she married is very successful and then she had kids. So we were already apart in experience but I thought we could still be friends. She was distancing herself and I didn't see it. She suffered from depression and stopped being the person she had been. She became mean-spirited and impatient with her kids, her friends. I was the one who

let go at that point because it made no sense to stay together. Decades later, this friend tried to reunite with me. I was reluctant but agreed. That was when I realized I was better off without her and I'm the one who put it to rest. We are not friends anymore.

Matilda, 34, living in Honolulu where she is a tour guide and recently married, tells us she has left friends because she knew there was "no good reason to stay."

> Sometimes I think about the two friends I stopped seeing. We were almost too close and it wasn't right. The world has changed since the pandemic. I began to rethink these friendships and I knew there was a problem and that we had a bad history. When we were younger we'd been involved with some bad things together. That was enough for me to feel like moving apart. There were issues about trust and about being real to one another. I miss having both friends but also I don't want to be caught in a web. Today I have my guard up when it comes to new friends. My sister and I are very close, that fills the need for a friend. I keep thinking of what our mother would have said and how she would have approved of what I did. She would say to lose both of them and I have.

Honing Our Skills

Though each of the women above are at varying stages of life, what they have in common is their ability to claim the estrangement with their once cherished female friends. For Renata, it is because she deeply offended her friend, for Becca, her friend has changed and is virtually unrecognizable and for Matilda, it is her self-awareness that brings her to a clean sweep when it comes to two of her friends.

These three narratives support the concept of taking charge and moving onward. If a friendship does not offer a secure, fruitful, trusting give and take, women today feel justified in being an estranger or estrangee.

In an essay by Vicki Levy and Collette Thayer, "Value, Depth and Age: The Prism of Today's Friendships," the authors found that nine out of ten adults feel that friends are "an essential part of living a healthy and happy life." They also report that almost half of all adults want a "more meaningful relationship with their close friends." Of those who feel this way, sixty-four percent are millennials and thirty-six percent are boomers.

If we consider how profound friendships among women are, then it is plausible that an estrangement, while liberating and brave, also deserves a time of grieving. Elisabeth Kubler-Ross, in her book, *On Death and Dying*, defines the five stages of grief as denial, anger, bargaining, depression and acceptance. Her model can apply to losses in life, not only to dying. That would include the cessation of a valued friendship, a job loss, a divorce, or family estrangement as well. When we are grieving, it is about losing someone we love and the end of that relationship.

As we have heard from the interviewees, these friendships have been significant. Remember when we looked at the 'medium friendships' as Lisa Miller labels them in her essay? These are not the friends who can devastate you, where the situation is unsustainable and estrangement is a solution. We're off the hook with a 'medium friend,' she isn't going to break your heart. Nor will she provide the sustenance and rapport that exists in an important, successful friendship, one where there is not disappointment or betrayal.

Let's look at how deeply wounded the following women are:

Gina, 38, a Physician's Assistant in an Urgent Care office, lives in New York with her husband and young daughter:

> Ten years ago my close friend and I were in the same rental summer house at the shore. What was weird from the start was how she didn't want me in that house. I was the one who had found the place and I was looking forward to a great summer. I thought we'd be together every weekend. Then she got everyone to agree that I should be asked to go and had me kicked out. She is mercenary for sure, but I also have no idea why she did this. We knew each other well and hung out all the time. After that summer, we stopped being friends. She wasn't talking to me. After she started everything I stopped trying to fix it, I wasn't talking to her either.
>
> When she got married she did not invite me and then I learned about it. When she heard about my wedding, she wanted to be part of it. She asked to be in it as if nothing had ever happened. We met for lunch after months of not seeing each other. I calmly explained. It was like breaking up with a boyfriend. I cared so much and yet I knew what she had done to me. I said no, there was no more friendship.

Another woman, Rory, became strong when she considered the pros and cons of remaining in a friendship that had turned substandard. At 37, Rory lives in Pittsburgh, where she is a financial advisor.

I'm better with my husband, our son and my sisters because of my real friends. We've been a support system since graduate school. I have friends who are not part of this and I'm not sure how they feel. I imagine they don't like it. There was one friend who was very special to me and turned out to be damaging. It took me an entire year but I'm over it and I've left her. I don't miss her at all. I don't think of her anymore. If we were in touch again, she would only be hurt by my feelings. I don't need her to judge everything. Why would I be with a girlfriend who makes me feel bad about myself? I have totally evolved.

Living with my husband and climbing a corporate ladder and being with solid girlfriends, I've learned my worth is most important. I don't love this friend. I don't need her. What we had is gone. What I learned is when you lose, you have to pick up your value and spend time with people who give back. It took me a while, but I don't want to be friends with anyone who isn't going to give me happiness.

Degrees of Separation

What I found is that our expectations often fuel our reactions to our female friends. As evidenced, women often avoid confrontation, they don't want to be alone or pushed out of the group. That is why our first inclination is to salvage the friendship, it's too threatening to leave. Others ask themselves if they can tolerate the friend for peace of mind. Or was it a circumstantial closeness all along and nothing more? Interviewees have noted there is no guarantee the next friendship won't have its own set of problems. It is what we have learned from the former friendship that enables us to go forward with healthy friendships.

In reaching the decisive moment, self-knowledge and self-confidence kick in. Instead of being uneasy and trapped, women are taking a stand, finally honest about their gains and losses with a specific friend. The more we face the circumstance, the better equipped we are to extricate ourselves. The following narratives illustrate the journey to estrangement with a valued friend.

For example, Gabby, 31, living in Delaware where she works as a florist, has flip-flopped over her best friend for the past three years:

> I go back and forth about my best friend. I am not sure of the future with her, still I can't let her go. Right now we are not talking but I can't decide if I want to talk to her again. If I listen to my instincts I do not want to be friends with her anymore. I can't depend on her and she has done a few terrible things to me. Each time she apologizes and I wonder if this is going to be our pattern. I know she is not a good person but I've spent years defending her and spending time with her. It's like having a bad boyfriend except at least I get rid of them after a while. I know what I want: friends who want to make friendships equal, friends that can give equal energy. That's what I'm looking for. I'm deciding if I should leave, I know I should.

In contrast is Sydney, 43, a publicist who lives in Indianapolis. She is single with children and has recently come to terms with the end of a best friendship.

> We were best friends for ten years, carrying each other through our two horrible divorces. We were supposed to be each other's protectors. I began to date one man I cared about and asked her if my two kids could spend

> the weekend with her, she said no. She told me I was selfish and she defended my ex. She said she understood why he wanted to get away from me. It was so unfair because she knew he had been abusive. Then she stopped talking to me and at first I was so worried but not now. Today, after a long haul, I want nothing to do with her. Maybe it's a mutual ending for us.

Cathy, 52, lives in Boston and works in retail. Like Sydney, she has severed her ties with a longtime friend:

> A few years ago my best friend and I broke up. We'd been hanging out together since fifth grade when she decided that my older brothers were so cool. She used me from the start but I wanted to be her friend, we ended up doing everything together for years, decades. Always we fought over who knew best—about the boys we liked as teenagers, the apartment we rented after college, the men we married. Who had the better job and the better life? We'd include each other or sometimes we'd be mean and go off with other friends without inviting each other. The reality is we were never supportive or nice enough. Finally I wanted out and so did she. It was mutual, kind of like a marriage that ends. We did talk about it and decided to take a break. But really we let it go totally—like being liberated.

Undaunted

It is worth noting the important changes in attitude toward leaving a failed friendship. Women are impressively open to estrangement compared to the past, moving toward self-reflection and a breather. As therapist Donna Laikind tells us, "What has happened in our families happens in friendships. But with family drama, even today, we try not to break up while with friends we are realizing we can." Lauren Mechling's piece in The *New York Times, How to End a Friendship,* addresses the fact that only enriching, balanced friendships add value. She writes of her experience with a friend, "… friendships are fragile, and most aren't built to last forever … that she and I made it through the better part of a decade was a feat."

Nicole, 59, living in southern Massachusetts where she works as a caregiver and has four adult children, views her path to estrangement as overdue and painful at first and later a source of strength:

> We were the closest friends for five years and every weekend we saw each other. We are the same age and our children are too. Originally we came from Portugal and we both take care of elderly people. But she never liked working and only wanted to have fun. She thought of herself as very beautiful and had a big ego. She would date men hoping they had money. It wasn't right or decent. I began to see who she really was. When she was on disability for an injury, her attitude about this surfaced. Everyone was helping her and cooking for her. She stopped thinking about work. She spent her days on social media while the women in our circle of friends were all working very hard. I told her she needed to get back to her job, that she wasn't kind to her daughters and made them pay for her. It isn't how we should treat our children. She was angry and accused me of talking about her. I had no respect for her.
>
> She made what I said into a war and I saw she was not someone I want for a friend. I was hurt at the start

because she stopped talking to me. I tried to work it out. She would have none of it. Now I'm fine with the fact she won't speak to me. If I met her today, I'd walk in the other direction.

When we endow a friend with qualities she doesn't have, as Nicole did, it comes as a shock when we discover the friend doesn't share our principles. Although we have come to know who the person is, it's still a loss when the friendship frays. As I write at the outset of this book, there is the question of how the friendships played out and who was responsible—perhaps both friends to varying degrees. Each of us has been an estranger or an estrangee at points of our lives. We have been at fault and we have been wronged.

As for my own personal journey with Paulette, the last time we were in touch was before Covid. We were at a mutual friend's father's funeral. We spoke briefly. She told me she was having a big party for her daughter who had just completed graduate school. I thought since I'd known her daughter since she was born and because Paulette described the party in detail and mentioned the date that I'd be invited. Yet I wasn't. A year or two later, when I was having a family celebration, the kind she would have been invited to in the past, I did not invite her. Are we on a par now, have we estranged each other? What I know is that it no longer matters. We are officially over and that in itself is sufficient. The hesitancy I felt for decades in our periods of togetherness and during our silences is gone. Since my encounters and the grand finale with Paulette, there have been other friendships that closed out in disappointment and pain. And working on this project for three years has triggered memories of those circumstances. In the magnitude of the interviews I have also found solace and proof that neither I, nor any of us, is alone in this.

While our goal is to not offend or let down a friend, as we have seen, there are multilevel wounds. Anything from duplicity and dishonesty to misdemeanors can harm the marrow of a female friendship. Determining when to leave the friend behind is within our grasp.

Estranged

Throughout this book a profound attachment to our female friends is apparent, despite serious challenges within the relationship. While historically women have been better at ending a marriage or a love affair than a complicated female friendship, this is now changing. Many women have honed their skills to disengage from a suboptimal situation. They are able to own what has happened in these friendships. If a friend has played a destructive role in one's life, rather than attempt to reconcile or renegotiate, estrangement becomes a chosen solution. Becoming estranged differs from the past.

While either side may long for the friend, we boldly face that estrangement could be a necessary step. We move ahead, toward self-discovery, personal survival, robust bonds and acceptance. In this manner, estranging offers women truth, hope and authenticity.

ACKNOWLEDGMENTS

To the women who came forward to share their deepest connections and struggles with their female friends, I offer a profound thank you. They cannot be thanked personally because identifying characteristics have been changed to insure confidentiality. Their narratives are the essence of this book.

Gratitude goes to: Jennifer Weis and Shannon O'Neil who offered great guidance and expertise, Alice Martell who listened early on to my interest in estrangement and the repercussions. Meryl Moss for her encouragement and ongoing belief in this project. Becky Stowe for her editorial skills, Sally McElwain for proofing, Cynthia Conrad and Deb Zipf at Meryl Moss Media and the entire team at Meridian Editions. The professionals who have contributed their thoughts to this book, Donald Cohen, Marion McCue de Velez, Donna Laikind, Diana Nash, Seth Shulman and Jeffrey Werden. Neil Rosini, wise attorney, and Max Brockman for his advice.

To my 'team': Treasured family and friends always, The Roosevelt Writing Group, Katie Schaffstall, Alexa Lieberthal, Howard Ressler for all of it.

QUESTIONNAIRE RESPONSES

In addition to the one hundred and fifty women whom I interviewed for *Estranged*, I conducted a survey. I received one hundred and eleven answers and the findings are below. As with the interviewees in the book, the respondents reflect a diverse group.

1. **Please state your age**

21-30:	18.02%
31-40:	28.83%
41-50:	21.62%
51-60:	15.32%
61-80:	16.22%

2. **Have you ever had a problem with a close friend?**

Yes	88.29%
No	11.71%

3. **If so, what sort of issue was it?**

You no longer trust her	41.44%
She has lied to you	21.62%
She has tried to take your boyfriend	4.5%
She has tried to take your ideas at work	4.5%
N/A	27.93%

4. If so, how many years have you been friends?

0-10	47.75%
11-20	32.43%
21-30	9.91%
31-40	9.91%

5. Was there one incident that changed everything?

Yes	74.77%
No	25.23%

6. If yes, can you offer details?

Icing you socially	12.61%
Choosing another friend over you	13.51%
Disparaged you	8.11%
A jealous act	21.62%
Other	29.73%
N/A	14.41%

7. Have you ever wanted to leave a friend behind?

Yes	67.57%
No	32.43%

8. If so, why?

No longer share same values	28.83%
You have moved on	24.32%
Your partner doesn't like her	2.7%
She insults you in public	9.01%
Other	13.51%
N/A	21.62%

9. Do you and your friend have different finances?
    Yes   77.48%
    No   22.52%

10. Are you secretly envious of your best friend's life?
    Yes   24.32%
    No   75.68%

11. What does your best friend have that appeals to you most?
    Husband   1.8%
    Lifestyle   25.23%
    Beauty   10.81%
    Children   5.41%
    Other   56.76%

12. What beliefs, if any, no longer fit with your best friend's?
    Politics   17.12%
    Religion   16.22%
    Drugs/Drinking   20.72%
    Money   10.81%
    Other   35.14%

13. Have you ever left a friend and felt relieved?
    Yes   75.68%
    No   24.32%

14. Have you ever been relieved when a friend leaves you?
    Yes   62.16%
    No   37.84%

15. Did a very close friend ever do something that deliberately hurt you?

    Yes   65.77%
    No   34.23%

16. Did you ever do something that deliberately hurt your close friend?

    Yes   32.43%
    No   67.57%

17. Do you have the courage to confront a friend over an issue?

    Yes   77.48%
    No   22.52%

18. Why would you stay with a friend if it was no longer a healthy friendship?

    Mutual friends   21.62%
    Past history   30.63%
    Secrets shared that can be incriminating   6.31%
    Loyalty   22.52%
    Other   18.92%

19. Do you believe the societal message is that our female friends are at the center of our happiness?

    Yes   32.43%
    No   30.63%
    Somewhat   36.94%

20. Are you truly happy for your friend's achievements?

    Yes   83.78%
    No   4.5%
    Somewhat   11.71%

21. What about her achievements cause you to have mixed feelings?

Physical appearance	9.91%
Career	7.21%
Lifestyle	20.72%
Men	6.31%
Children	0.90%
Money	8.11%
N/A	46.85%

22. Could you be close to a best friend whose path has veered from yours?

Yes	80.18%
No	19.82%

23. Have you ever done something terrible to your friend?

Yes	23.42%
No	76.58%

24. Have you ever had a friend who has done something terrible to you?

Yes	61.26%
No	38.74%

25. What would cause you to leave a meaningful friendship?

Unfairness	26.13%
Being excluded	30.63%
Political differences	4.5%
Other reason	35.14%

26. **What do you expect from your friendship that is missing from the relationship?**

Prioritizing the friendship	14.41%
Loyalty	22.52%
The truth	26.13%
Being inclusive	13.51%
Other reason	23.42%

27. **Breaking up with a female friend takes courage. Have you done it?**

Yes	72.97%
No	27.03%

28. **Has anyone broken up with you?**

Yes	63.06%
No	36.94%

29. **Is your point of view that we are obligated to stay with a female friend more than with a male partner or husband if we are not comfortable with the relationship?**

Yes	75.68%
No	24.32%

30. **Do you believe that becoming estranged from a friend has been a positive solution for you?**

Yes	79.28%
No	20.72%

31. **Have you ever reconnected with a friend whom you have severed ties?**

Yes	71.17%
No	28.83%

REFERENCES

"All Things Considered." NPR, 27 October 2020.

American Perspectives Study, Survey Center on American Life, 2023.

And Just Like That. Created by Darren Star, Michael Patrick King Productions, HBO Entertainment, Pretty Matches Productions, Rialto Films, 2021-2023.

Atwood, Margaret. *Cat's Eye*. 1st Anchor books pbk. ed. New York, Anchor Books, 1998.

Banks, A., Hirschman, L.A. and Siegel, D. Wired to Connect: *The Surprising Link Between Brain Science and Strong, Healthy Relationships*. Penguin Publishing Group; Reprint edition, 2016.

Barash, S.S. *Toxic Friends: The Antidote for Women Stuck in Complicated Friendships*. St. Martin's Press; First Edition, 13 October 2009.

Barash, S. S. *Tripping the Prom Queen: The Truth About Women and Rivalry*. St. Martin's Press, 2007.

Barash, S.S. *You're Grounded Forever…But First, Let's Go Shopping: The Challenges Mothers Face with Their Daughters and Ten Timely Solutions*. St. Martin's Press; First Edition, 28 September 2010.

Barb & Star Go to Vista Del Mar. Directed by Josh Greenbaum, Lionsgate, 2021.

Barbie. Directed by Greta Gerwig, Warner Bros. Pictures, 2023.

Beauvoir, Simone de, 1908-1986. *The Second Sex*. London: Jonathan Cape, 2009.

Beck, J. "How Friendships Change in Adulthood." *The Atlantic*, 22 October 2015.

Bell, P. "Our Expectations Of Millennial Friendships Don't Prepare Us For The Reality." *Refinery 29*, 2019. https://www.refinery29.com/en-gb/2019/12/8725819/importance-of-female-friendships

Berkowitz, G. "Study on Friendship Among Women." *UCLA*, 1998.

Blieszner, Rosemary et al. "Friendship in Later Life: A Research Agenda." *Innovation in aging* vol. 3,1 igz005. 30 Mar. 2019, doi:10.1093/geroni/igz005

Bride Wars. Directed by Gary Winick, 20th Century Fox, 2009.

Bridgerton. Created by Chris Van Dusen, Shondaland, CVD Productions, 2020-2024.

Brooks, D. "What Is It About Friendships That Is So Powerful?" *The New York Times*, 4 August 2022.

Cacioppo, S. & Araya, J.L. *Wired for Love: A Neuroscientist's Journey Through Romance, Loss, and the Essence of the Human Connection*. Unabridged. [New York], Macmillan Audio, 2022.

Caruso, S. "All about the vanderpump rules cheating drama involving Tom Sandoval, Ariana Madix and Raquel Leviss." *People Magazine*, 2023.

Cherry, K. "Horney's Theory of Neurotic Needs." *Very Well Mind*, 2023 March 15.

Cinderella. Directed by Kay Cannon, Columbia Pictures, Fullwell 73, 2021.

Cline, Emma. *The Girls: A Novel*. First edition. New York, Random House, 2016.

Collins, N.L. and Miller, L.C. "Self-Disclosure and Liking: A Meta-Analytical Review." *Psychological Bulletin*, Vol. 116, No. 3, 457-475, 1994.

Crawford, R. *A Song for You: My Life With Whitney Houston*, Dutton, 2019.

Cunningham, Michael R., and Barbee, Anita P. "Relationship Conflict." *Close Relationships: A Sourcebook,* edited by Clyde Hendrick and Susan S. Hendrick, Sage Publications, November 2001.

Dainton, M., Zelley, E. & Langan, E. *Maintaining Relationships Through Communication: Relational, Contextual, and Cultural Variations.* New York, Routledge, 2003.

Daly, Paula. *Keep Your Friends Close.* Grove Press, 2014.

D'Costa D'Silva, M. "Should you date your BFF's Sibling?" *DNA India,* 2018 June 18.

Degges-White, S. "When Friends Reveal Secrets You've Asked Them to Keep." *Psychology Today,* 25 May 2014.

Denson TF, O'Dean SM, Blake KR & Beames JR. "Aggression in Women: Behavior, Brain and Hormones." Frontiers, 2 May 2018.

Desperate Housewives. Created by Marc Cherry, Cherry Productions, ABC Studios, 2004-2012.

Dindia, K., & Allen, M. "Sex differences in self-disclosure: A meta-analysis." Psychological Bulletin, 112(1), 1992, 106–124. https://doi.org/10.1037//0033-2909.112.1.106

Dolan, Paul, The Science Behind Happiness, website. 2023

Donnellan, S. "Tiffani Thiessen and Jennie Garth Reunite at Bethenny Frankel's Dinner Party After Feud." *Us Weekly,* 18 October 2023.

Dunbar, Robin. *Friends: Understanding the Power of Our Most Important Relationships,* Little Brown, UK, April 2022.

80 for Brady. Directed by Kyle Marvin, Paramount Pictures, 2023.

"Elizabeth Keckley." Virginia Museum of History and Culture.

Ferrante, E, Goldstein, A, *My Brilliant Friend*, Europa Editions, 2012

Fisher, H.E. "The Tyranny of Love: Love Addiction—An Anthropologist's View." Behavioral Addictions, *Academic Press*, 2014, Pages 237-265, ISBN 9780124077249, https://doi.org/10.1016/B978-0-12-407724-9.00010-0.

Freedman, G, Powell, D.N, Le, B. & Williams, K.D. "Ghosting and Destiny: Implicit theories of relationships predict beliefs about ghosting," Journal of Social and Personal Relationships, 2019.

Friends. Created by David Crane and Marta Kauffman, Bright/Kauffman/Crane Productions, Warner Bros. Television, 1994-2004.

Friends With Money. Directed by Nicole Holofcener, Sony Pictures Classic, 2006.

Fromm, E. *The Art of Loving*. Allen & Unwin, 1958.

Fuller, K. "The Importance of Female Friendships Among Women." *Psychology Today*, 16 August 2018.

Gaitskill, M. "The Friendship Challenge." *The New Yorker*, 5 February 2024.

General Federation of Women's Clubs (GFWC), United States of America.

Goddard, I. "What does friendship look like in America?" *Pew Research Center*, 12 October 2023.

Good Girls. Created by Jenna Bans, Minnesota Logging Company, Universal Television, 2018-2021.

Grace and Frankie. Created by Marta Kauffman and Howard J. Morris, Skydance Television, 2015-2022.

Gramlich, John. "Nearly half of Americans have a family member or close friend who's been addicted to drugs." Pew Research Center, 26 October 2017.

Hannah, Kristin. *Firefly Lane.* 1st St. Martin's Griffin ed. New York, St. Martin's Griffin, 2009.

Hawken, L. "What happened to Jessica Mulroney after she was ditched by Meghan Markle? From social media digs at the Duchess to lost television work for stylist who played starring role at the royal wedding." *Daily Mail Online,* 24 February 2024.

Heditsian, X. "Coming Back From and Breaking the Cycle of Toxic Fighting in Your Relationship." Naya Clinics.

Holland, M. *Social Bonding & Nurture Kinship: Compatibility between cultural and biological approaches*, Createspace Independent Publishing, 2012.

Hyde, J. S., & Kling, K. C. "Women, Motivation, and Achievement." *Psychology of Women Quarterly.* 2001, 25(4), 364–378.

Igoe, K. J. "32 of the Most Legendary Hollywood Rivalries." *Marie Claire,* 16 February 2024.

Ingo, K.M., Mize, K.D. and Pratarelli, M.E. "Female Intrasexual Competition: Toward an Evolutionary Feminist Theory." *Theory and Science,* 2007.

Johnson, F & Aries, E.J. "The talk of women friends." *Women's Studies International Forum*, Volume 6, Issue 4, 1983, Pages 353-361, ISSN 0277-5395, https://doi.org/10.1016/0277-5395(83)90027-4.

Kashdan, T. "Why Are You Rethinking Friendships Because of Politics?" *Psychology Today,* 29 September 2020.

Kashner, S. "The Complicated Sisterhood of Jackie Kennedy and Lee Radziwill." *Vanity Fair,* 26 April 2016.

Keckley. E. *Behind the Scenes: Or, Thirty Years a Slave, and Four Years in the White House*. Eno Publishers, April 4, 2016.

Kelner, J., & Gavriel-Fried, B. (2023). "'The relationship changed because I had changed': Experiences and perceptions of friendships between women treated for substance use disorder in women-only residential programs." *Feminism & Psychology, 33*(4), 647-667. https://doi.org/10.1177/09593535231176349

Kettler, S. "Ella Fitzgerald and Marilyn Monroe: Inside their surprising friendship," *Biography.com*, 15 September 2020, (n.d.-a).

Kimmel, M. *The Gendered Society*. Oxford University Press; 6th edition, 1 July 2016.

Kirsch, M. "We Can't All Be BFFs. Enter the 'Medium Friend.'" *New York Times*, 31 August 2024.

Kubler-Ross, E. *On Death and Dying: What the Dying Have to Teach Doctors, Nurses, Clergy and Their Own Families*. Scribner Reissue, 12 August 2014.

Kuhn, P.J. & Villeval, M.C. "Are Women More Attracted to Cooperation Than Men?" National Bureau of Economic Research, 2013.

Lalot, F. "The unkindest cut of all: A quantitative study of betrayal narratives." *Journal of Community & Applied Social Psychology, 2023, 33*(6), 1580–1601.

Larsen, Nella. *Passing*. New York, Penguin Classics, 2003.

Legally Blonde. Directed by Robert Luketic, Metro-Goldwyn-Mayer Pictures, Marc Platt Productions, Type A Films, 2001.

Levy, V. & Thayer, C. "Value, Depth and Age: The Prism of Today's Friendships." AARP, 2020.

Lopate, P. "On the Death of Friendship." *The American Scholar*, 2 June 2017.

Macdonald, G., and Leary., M.R. "Why does social exclusion hurt? The relationship between social and physical pain." *Psychological bulletin* vol. 131,2 (2005): 202-23. doi:10.1037/0033-2909.131.2.202

Maslow, A. H. "A Dynamic Theory of Human Motivation," *Psychological Review*, 2022, 26–47. https://doi.org/10.1037/11305-004

Mazzella, R. "How to navigate A (friendship) threesome." The Girlfriend, 26 May 2020.

McBeth, Colette, Precious Thing. New York, Minotaur Books, 2014.

Mead, M. *Blackberry winter: My earlier years*. Kodansha International, 1995.

Mean Girls. Directed by Mark Waters, Paramount Pictures, 2004.

Mechling, L. *How Could She*. Viking, 2019.

Mechling, L. "How to End a Friendship." *The New York Times*, 14 June 2019.

Messud, C. *The Woman Upstairs*. Knopf Doubleday Publishing Group; Reprint edition, 2014.

Miller, L. "The Vexing Problem of the 'Medium Friend.'" *The New York Times,* 22 June 2024.

Moore, L. *Who Will Run the Frog Hospital?: A Novel* A.A. Knopf, 1994.

Moriarty, L. *Big Little Lies*. New York, NY, HBO Home Entertainment, 2017.

Morrison, T. *Sula*. Vintage, 1998.

Moving On. Directed by Paul Weitz, Roadside Attractions, 2023.

Murphy, K. "Do Your Friends Actually Like You?" *The New York Times,* 6 August 2016.

National Alternative Dispute Resolution Advisory Council. "Alternative Dispute Resolution Definitions." Canberra: The Council, 1997.

Nehring, S.M., Chen, R.J., & Freeman, A.M. "Alcohol Use Disorder." National Library of Medicine, StatPearls Publishing, 2024.

9 to 5. Directed by Colin Higgins, 20th Century Fox, 1980.

"Not All Things are Black and White: Elizabeth Taylor and Debbie Reynolds." *ElizabethTaylor.com*, 2023.

Parvez, H. "Why betrayal of friends hurts so much." *Psych Mechanics*, 13 July 2024.

Pawlowski, A. *"Marriage Can be Lonely: Why it Happens and What to Do."* TODAY.com, 15 June 2020.

Pearce, E., Machin, A., & Dunbar, R. I. "Sex Differences in Intimacy Levels in Best Friendships and Romantic Partnerships." *Adaptive Human Behavior and Physiology*, 2020, 7(1), 1–16. https://doi.org/10.1007/s40750-020-00155-z

Perrault, Charles, 1628-1703. *Cinderella.* Scarsdale, N.Y.: Bradbury Press, 19731972.

Poppe, G. "The Harsh Reality Of Losing Your Best Friend To Their Boyfriend." *Your Tango*, 21 May 2021.

Reynolds, T. A. "Our Grandmothers' Legacy: Challenges Faced by Female Ancestors Leave Traces in Modern Women's Same-Sex Relationships." *Archives of Sexual Behavior*, 51(7), 2021, 3225–3256. https://doi.org/10.1007/s10508-020-01768-x

Rubin, L.B. *Just Friends: The Role of Friendship in Our Lives.* New York, Harper & Row, 1985.

Satow, R. "How Friendships Evolve Throughout the Life Cycle." *Psychology Today*, 2 April 2021. https://www.psychologytoday.com/us/blog/life-after-50/202104/how-friendships-evolve-throughout-the-life-cycle

Schlissel, L. *Women's Diaries of the Westward Journey.* New York, Schocken Books, 1982.

Sex in the City. Created by Darren Star, Darren Star Productions, HBO Entertainment, 1998-2004.

Shakespeare in Love. Milano. Panorama. (1998).

Simmel, G. "The Sociology of Secrecy and of Secret Societies." *American Journal of Sociology,* 1906, 11(4), 441–498. https://doi.org/10.1086/211418

Single White Female. Directed by Barbet Schroeder, Columbia Pictures, 1992

Smith, Zadie. *Swing Time.* First large print edition. [New York, New York], Random House Large Print in association with Penguin Press, an imprint of Penguin Random House LLC, 2016.

Someone Great. Directed by Jennifer Kaytin Robinson, Feigco Entertainment, Likely Story, I Can & I Will Productions, 2019.

Sow, A. & Friedman, A. *Big Friendship: How We Keep Each Other Close.* First Simon & Schuster trade paperback edition. New York, Simon & Schuster Paperbacks, 2021.

Spiotta, D. *Innocents and Others: A Novel.* First Scribner hardcover edition, Scribner, 2016.

Staff, American Addictions Center. "Signs & symptoms of addiction (Physical & Mental)." *American Addiction Centers,* 29, July 2024.

Staff, MIT Media Lab. "Friendship Reciprocity and Behavioral Change." MIT Media Lab, August 2016.

Staff, "Madonna and Gwyneth Paltrow in Shocking Friend Breakup!" *New York Magazine,* 10 June 2010.

Staff, Us Weekly. "Celebrity Best Friend Breakups: Stars Who Ended Their Friendships." *Us Weekly,* 3 October 2023.

Staff, Us Weekly. "Gwyneth Paltrow: 'I Can Be Mean' and 'Harbor Revenge.'" *Us Weekly*, 6 April 2010.

Staff, Us Weekly. "Taylor Swift's Celebrity BFFs through the Years: Photos." *Us Weekly*, 26 July 2024.

Stage Door. Directed by Gregory La Cava, RKO Radio Pictures, 1937.

Sternberg, Robert, J., "Triangular Theory of Love." *Psychological Review*, 1986.

Sussex Publishers. (n.d.-a). *How friendships evolve throughout the life cycle*. Psychology Today. https://www.psychologytoday.com/us/blog/life-after-50/202104/how-friendships-evolve-throughout-the-life-cycle

Sussex Publishers. (n.d.-b). *The importance of female friendships among women*. Psychology Today. https://www.psychologytoday.com/us/blog/happiness-is-state-mind/201808/the-importance-female-friendships-among-women

Sussex Publishers. (n.d.-c). *Why are you rethinking friendships because of politics?*. Psychology Today. https://www.psychologytoday.com/us/blog/curious/202009/why-are-you-rethinking-friendships-because-politics

Sweet Magnolias. Directed by Herbert Ross, Tri-Star Pictures, 1989.

Tanasugarn, A. "What Really Drives Ghosting in Relationships." *Psychology Today*, 3 December 2023.

Tannen, D. "When Friends Are 'Like Family.'" *The New York Times*, 25 March 2016.

Taylor, S. E. "The Tending Instinct: Women, Men, and the Biology of Nurturing." Henry Holt and Co., 2003.

Towers, A. "Sarah Jessica Parker explains why Kim Cattrall wasn't invited to star in *And Just Like That*." *Entertainment Weekly*, 2 June 2022.

Traister, R. "What Women Find in Friends That They May Not Get from Love." The New York Times, 27 February 2016.

Veniegas, R.C. and Peplau, L A, "Power and the Quality of Same-Sex Friendships." Psychology of Women Quarterly, Volume 21, Issue 2, 1997.

Wainwright, H. "Winona Ryder and Gwyneth Paltrow's brutal friendship break-up is the stuff of Hollywood legend." *MamaMia.com*, 4 September 2024.

Weiner, J. *Big Summer*. Atria Books, 2021

Welsh McNulty, A. "Don't underestimate the power of women supporting each other at work." Harvard Business Review, 2018. https://hbr.org/2018/09/dont-underestimate-the-power-of-women-supporting-each-other-at-work

Whitaker, H. *"Is competition in female friendship the last taboo?"* Grazia, Updated on10 September 2019, https://graziadaily.co.uk/life/opinion/competitive-female-friendships/

Winfrey, Oprah. "Interview With Melinda French Gates." *Moments That Make Us: How Friendship Helped Oprah Winfrey & Gayle King Navigate Life's Big Changes*, 24 July 2024.

Wong, K. "Your Friend Has More Money Than You Do. How Can Your Relationship Survive?" The New York Times, 1 October 2024.

Working Girl. Directed by Mike Nichols, 20th Century Fox, 1988.

Young, K. "When Someone You Love has an Addiction." *Hey Sigmund*, 2024.

THE AUTHOR

SUSAN SHAPIRO BARASH has written over a dozen non-fiction books including *Tripping the Prom Queen, Toxic Friends* and *You're Grounded Forever, but First Let's Go Shopping*. For more than twenty years she taught gender studies in the Writing Seminar Department at Marymount Manhattan College and has guest taught creative nonfiction at the Writing Institute at Sarah Lawrence College. Her fiction, *A Palm Beach Wife* and *Maribelle's Shadow*, among other titles, is published under her pen name, Susannah Marren.

READER'S GUIDE

Questions for Discussion for *Estranged*

1. The author identifies seven classic scenarios with our female friends and how these relationships affect us. What situation is most familiar to you?

2. The stats at the beginning of the book include the following findings: 88% of women have had a problem with a close friend, 63% have had a friend breakup with them and 67% have wanted to leave a friend behind. Would you say you are part of any of these statistics and why?

3. Do you believe you've looked the other way in a friendship that has been unsatisfying or troubling? Are you aware of your reasons for this choice?

4. There are sister stories in this book as well. Do you have a sister and has there been drama along the way?

5. Throughout the book women of all ages describe hanging on to a friendship that is failing and unhappy. Have you found yourself doing this and why?

6. The author posits that some female friendships, as important as they are, have an expiration date. Would you agree that we are conditioned to believe female friendships should last forever?

7. Discuss what has come between you and a meaningful friend. Was it over your partner, your values, your politics—something else?

8. There are profound stories of female friendships on the brink despite that they were once secure. Did you and your friend share a conversation about this?

9. Although these friendships begin on a high note, there can be an ebbing of trust and sincerity over time. Has this caught you off guard?

10. The author writes about the "estrangee," who is dropped by her friend and the "estranger," who instigates the end of the friendship. Have you been at either end and how did it play out?

11. There are interviewees who share that their mothers were friends as well—and how it impacts their friendship. Have you ever experienced this?

12. The author's research uncovers disappointment and betrayal in female friendships. Would you agree that the decision to estrange is liberating? Do you view it as useful and necessary?

13. The narratives throughout the book are varied and emotional. Are there parts of the book that you would recommend to friends and family?

14. What has this book taught you? Have the sections at the end of each chapter offered insight?

15. After extensive research and interviews, the author believes that estrangement can be a powerful tool for women stuck in unproductive friendships. Do you find this illuminating?

RECOMMENDED FOR READERS OF *ESTRANGED*

An intimate look at the reasons women in monogamous relationships and marriages take a lover. In Susan Shapiro Barash's trailblazing book, women confide how they balance the emotional and physical aspects of their trysts.

Through personal accounts of over 70 women in their 20s to their 80s, we get a close-up picture of how women choose a lover as a form of self-exploration and agency.

A Passion for More reveals:

- ▶ How having a lover helps a woman to remain in an unhappy marriage or relationship,
- ▶ How women renegotiate a marriage/monogamous relationship after the affair,
- ▶ How an affair can improve one's marriage/monogamous relationship,
- ▶ How an affair is often the catalyst to leave a marriage/longstanding relationship.

www.ingramcontent.com/pod-product-compliance
Lightning Source LLC
Chambersburg PA
CBHW031613280325
24255CB00012B/32/J